# *Songs of the Earth* (1972-2021)
## Exhibition Catalogue

Roger Peters

*Songs of the Earth* (1972-2021)

**Exhibition Catalogue**

*In effect,*
*they could be regarded*
*as metaphors on existence,*
*on interpersonal relationships*
*as well as being*
*artistic endeavours*
*and propositions about art.*
*17th Sept. '72*

# Other titles by Roger Peters

*William Shakespeare's Sonnet Philosophy*
(Four volume, slipcase set – 2005)

*Volume 1*
How Shakespeare structures
his nature-based philosophy into the *Sonnets*
before he publishes them in 1609
(*Volume 1*, second edition – 2019)

*Volume 2*
A line by line analysis
of the 154 individual sonnets using
the *Sonnet* philosophy
as the basis for their meaning
(*Volume 2*, second edition – 2018)

*Volume 3*
An analysis of individual plays and poems
to show that the *Sonnet* philosophy
is the basis for their meaning
(*Volume 3*, second edition – 2020)

*Volume 4*
How the works of
Wittgenstein, Duchamp, and Mallarmé
led to an appreciation
of Shakespeare's philosophy
(*Volume 4*, second edition – 2019)

*Shakespeare's Global Philosophy* (2017)
exploring Shakespeare's nature-based
philosophy in the sonnets, plays and Globe

*Shakespeare & Mature Love* (2017)
how to get from nature to love in Shakespeare

*Shakespeare's Philosophy Illustrated* (2018)
Quaternary teaching aids

*Quaternary Essays* (2020)
applying Shakespeare's nature-based Sonnet
philosophy to life and art

QUATERNARY IMPRINT

Published for the Quaternary Institute

# CONTENTS

# *Songs of the Earth* (1972-2021)

The Installation of twenty-eight art works exhibited at Pihama Lavender in Coastal South Taranaki in May 2021 under the title *Songs of the Earth (1972 – 2021)* by Roger Peters marks the culmination of a fifty-year project begun at the Elam School of Art in Auckland in 1972.

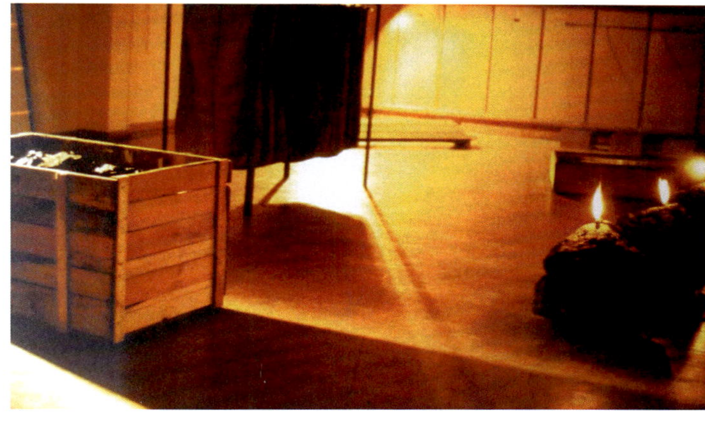

Having moved from the School of Architecture to Elam in 1971, it was in the Sculpture Department under Jim Allen in the August of the following year that the first installation titled *Being in a Space* was exhibited in the Lecture Theatre. The showing comprised works such as *Rocks, Red Ladder, Oil Bath, Coal Box, Sack Rack*, and *Ramp*. The 1972 installation was later entered in the Univerisities Arts Festival exhibition and won the Air New Zealand Award judged by Colin McCahon.

The move from achieving moderately successful grades during the three years at the School of Architecture – and in the first year at Elam – to getting a National Award in art in the second year felt both completely surprising and oddly unexceptional. After the birth of daughter Talia in April of 1972, I found myself experiencing an elevated sense of purpose and insight.

While my work was in conformity with the modernist program introduced to Elam by Jim Allen and others, my resolve to plumb the depths of understanding and expression meant sublimating the various influences to produce work with as much personal integrity as possible. Notes written in June and September of 1972 attest to the inordinate and somewhat gauche commitment.

The first is a handwritten statement penned two months after the birth of daughter Talia and two months before the Installation of *Being in a Space* at Elam. Then, a month after *Being in a Space*, I typed out the second resolution.

*Sunday 11th June (1972). I feel strange tensions indeed. My world is not of this, it is not of these riches and finery, these half-seen battles, these tried modes. I have no other desire than to get to basic experience (an infinite goal as any). How mundane yet how profound could it be to do well a simple task – to know that one way leaves chance in its way while to learn the rules, to observe the experienced would leave chance in its wake and open the path to far extended opportunities. To exist in a state that is only half true, to be a romantic of the old (to long for how was) is not for me. I need the reality, the closeness, the tensions indeed of an untried path, of a possible new angle on this real mystic world….. Tuesday 13.6.72: …. How to translate a philosophical notion to a plastic means. If I want to express meaninglessness, ambiguity, I need to establish a plastic vocabulary. If I want to let the piece have its own validity and not be dependent upon my doubts I must ensure that my doubts are of an order befitting my intentions. To be ruthless in eliminating misadventure – to be the mutant of chance not the victim, to turn chance to good fortune – to die eventually.*

In 1973, the third year at the Art School and the second year in the Sculpture Department, a group of art works titled *Common Ground* was displayed in the Lecture Theatre. Included were *Hot Wires*, *Snow*, *Waves*, *Wind*, *Pink*, *Netting*, *Salt*, and an early form of *Trees*. As with *Being in a Space*, a number of the works were highly energised while some were more passive serving as space dividers as well as adding points of connectivity across the whole Installation — as the title *Common Ground* suggests.

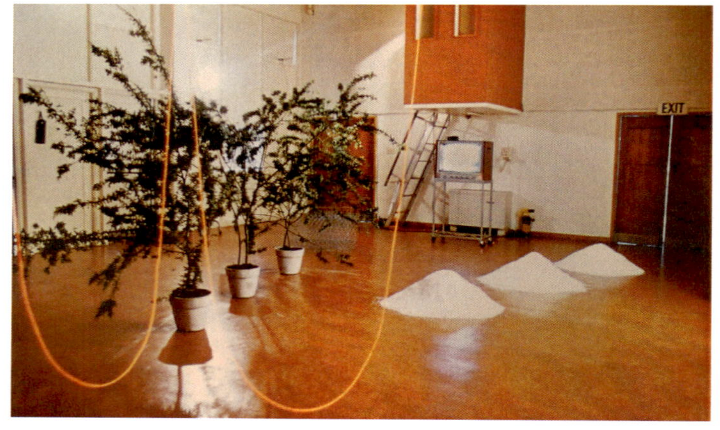


All eight works in *Common Ground* of 1973 participated to some degree in the aesthetics of the Installation with all the works being exhibited in *Songs of the Earth (1972-2021)* at Pihama either unchanged or somewhat modified. Of the eight works in the earlier 1972 Installation *Being in a Space*, two were unresolvable at the time and are no longer part of the overall aesthetic dynamic.

The greater resolution evident in *Common Ground* after *Being in a Space*, however, could not be sustained. Of the eight works in the 1974 Installation *Given Time* only three — *Blue Ladder*, *Slab* and *Fire* — have survived after the exhibition in the Lecture Theatre at Elam. Even back then, the title *Given Time* on one hand referred to the non-spatial nature of all aesthetic effects in the mind but also to the growing consciousness time would be needed to assess and resolve an impending creative impasse.

One consequence of the method of working developed from the middle of 1972 was that once an artwork was fully realised using a particular material or resource interest then shifted to another material or resource to similarly plumb its aesthetic potential. Hence, all the works are different albeit fired by the same aesthetic sensibility — which gives them their peculiar inter-relatability.

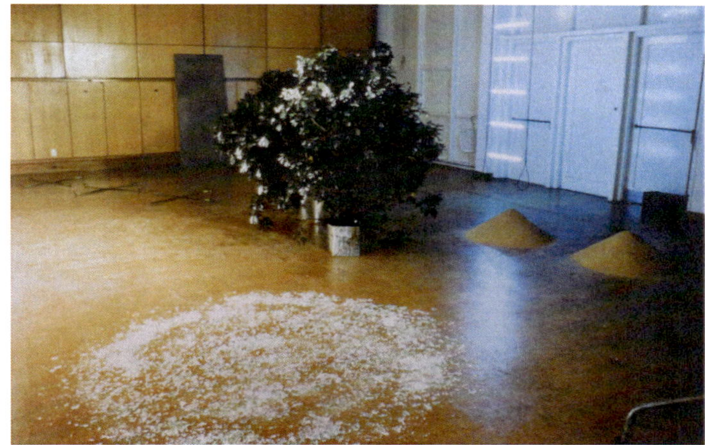

Then, as now, each time a material or resource presents as an aesthetic opportunity, it takes months of deliberation and exploration of the material's inherent characteristics and endless configurations before the final shape became evident – usually after a chance occurrence. The final form of the artwork as a recognisable ladder, wheel, etc., is only arrived at after the lengthy investigation and resolution process.

In the year after graduating from Elam, works from the previous three years were included in the Project Program series at the Auckland City Art Gallery. Each artist could use the gallery space for two weeks to install or perform their work.

In the end, the group of works under the title *Songs of the Earth* comprised nine previous works and one new one – *Rings*. While the idea was to create more new works for the Project Program Installation, the lacunae in inspiration experienced in the last year at Elam persisted with a few works in progress not being realised.

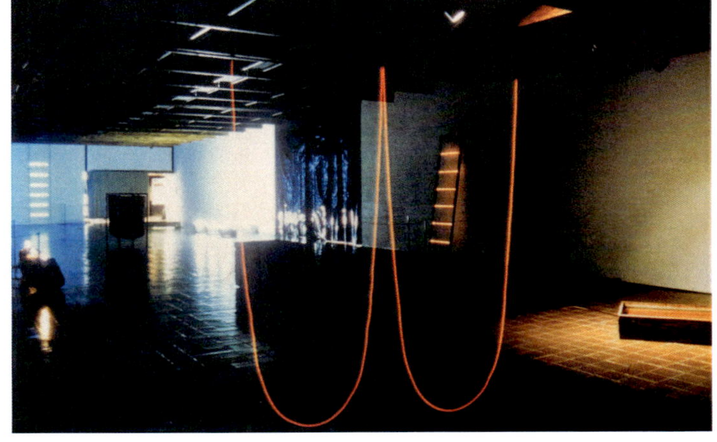

Over the next couple of years, while working out of a studio in a large industrial building in Parnell, a further two works were created. The *Wheel* of 1976 and the *Trees* of 1977 emerged from the familiar process of locating a material or resource, spending months over the gestation until the final form was realised.

With the exception of *Hot Wires*, the other artworks created over the period 1972 to 1977 had shapes like or close to familiar objects. The completely unexpected anthropomorphism of the *Hot Wires* – which revealed itself only after the work was turned on for the first time – enhanced the aesthetic dynamic of the other works.

Only when a piece of pink neon took my attention, and I began to explore its expressive possibilities, did the insistence of the anthropomorphic assert itself in the early stages of the investigation and expectation. Moreover, the pink neon persistently elicited the expressive form of a large penis.

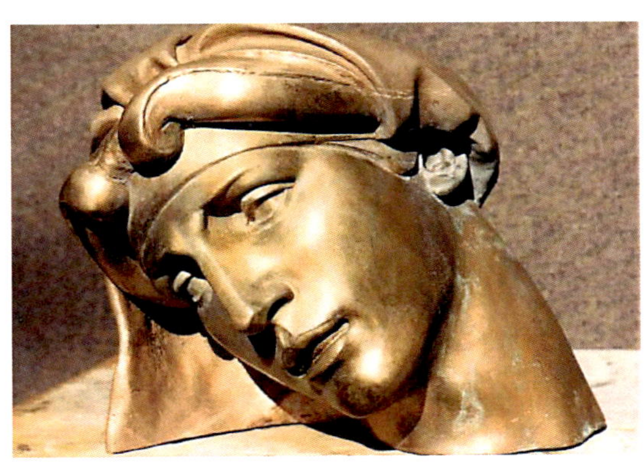

With the birth of a second daughter Teresa in 1978 to partner Maree Horner and a resolve to move to the countryside to live, the end of the 1970s brought about two resolutions. The first was to teach myself figurative sculptural skills to better explore the anthropomorphic suggestivity of the pink neon. The second was to do an intensive study of Marcel Duchamp to understand what enabled him to create works with total consistency of expression and aesthetic depth throughout his lifetime, albeit limited in number.

After seven years of study into the minds of not only Duchamp, but also Ludwig Wittgenstein, Stephane

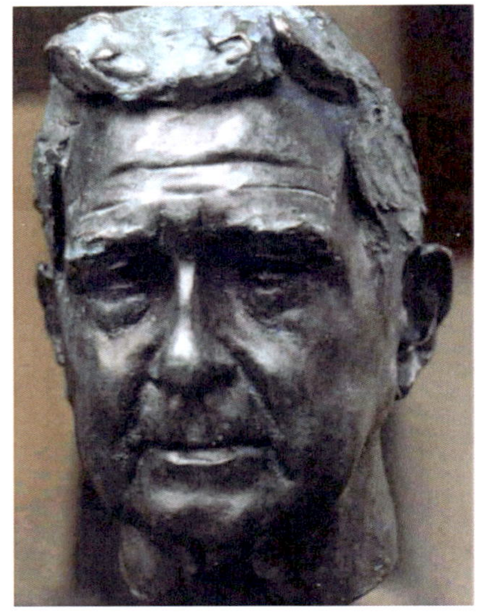

Mallarme and Charles Darwin and many other lesser artists, thinkers and writers in the untrammelled air of South Taranaki, in 1987 I wrote out a rudimentary philosophic tract titled *Human Being* and had copies printed. I felt I had, in essence, resolved the philosophic issues arising from the 1970s artistic explorations.

I then began a similar seven-year investigation into significant figurative art from over the Centuries while teaching myself the rudiments of modelling and bronze casting. This resulted in sporadic exhibitions of sculptured busts in bronze, plaster and concrete and the exploration of spaces and buildings using small figures in plasticine culminating in a Dome Show at the Sarjeant Gallery in Wanganui in 1994.

The two lines of investigation reached their apogee in Wanganui – by chance the town where I was born. On frequent trips to Wanganui I began attending a monthly Shakespeare group that read the plays aloud until in 1995 they decided to read Shakespeare's 154 sonnets over a weekend. As the reading progressed, I began to apprehend a profound nature-based female/

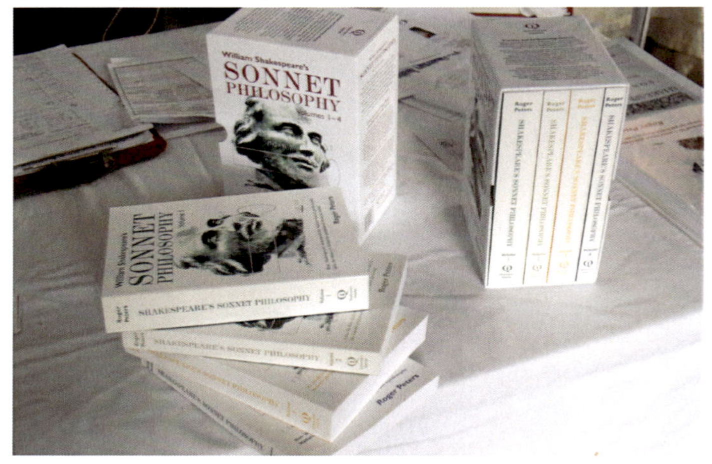

male-validating philosophy embedded in the set of sonnets that corresponded to the more rudimentary philosophic understanding I had developed by 1987.

I knew intuitively I was faced with the most comprehensive and consistent philosophy ever written that overarched the more specialised deliberations of Duchamp, Wittgenstein and Darwin, and everybody else. Moreover, as I cast around in academia and elsewhere world-wide I came to realise no one else in 400 years had come anywhere near appreciating much less verbalising Shakespeare's incredible achievement.

Consequently, by the year 2000, I inaugurated an entirely new level of advanced learning and insight beyond anything available in Tertiary. In keeping with the trajectory Primary, Secondary and Tertiary, I called the pedagogical development the Quaternary under the auspices of the Quaternary

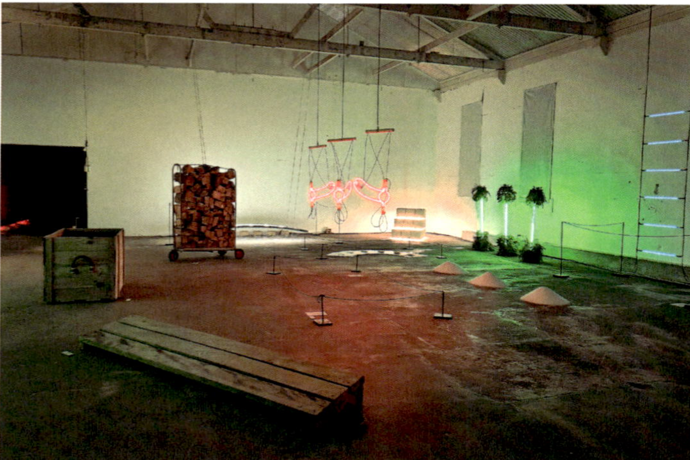

Institute (and website).

By 2005, a 1760-page four-volume 600,000-word slipcase set *William Shake-speare's Sonnet Philosophy* was published by Quaternary Imprint to detail the philosophy of the 1609 *Sonnets* as the philosophy behind Shakespeare's thirty-six plays in the 1623 *Folio* and his four longer poems. The fourth Volume considered the contributions of the proto-Quaternary thinkers, etc., I had studied for years.

Since 2005, Quaternary Imprint has published *Shakespeare's Global Philosophy*

(2017), *Shakespeare & Mature Love* (2017), *Shakespeare's Philosophy Illustrated* (2018), re-published *William Shakespeare's Sonnet Philosophy* in hardback and paperback (2018 – 2020), and *Quaternary Essays* (2020). Forthcoming is a 900-page, 800,000-word commentary around the thirty-six plays in the 1623 *Folio* - plus other incidental publications.

In 2017, with the Shakespeare findings and related material either published or about to be, I decided to recreate the artworks of the 1970s. With some works or parts of works still extant, and with a desire to revisit the pink neon shape of the late 1970s, I began envis-

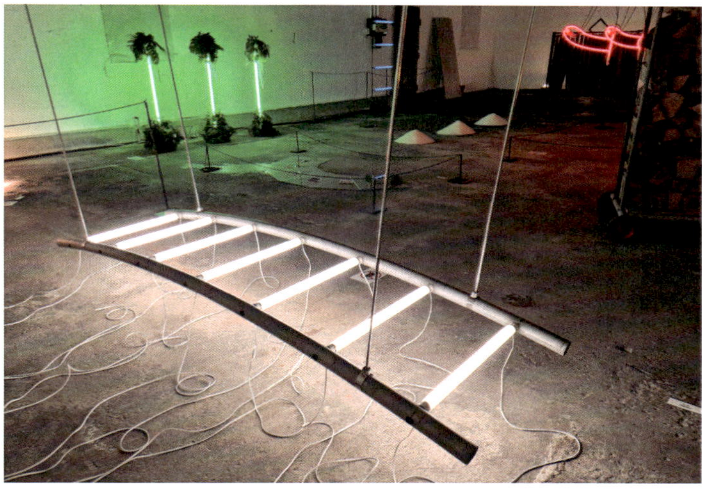

aging an installation of around eighteen or so artworks from the 1970s. As the project developed and new ideas emerged the total number of works eventually became twenty eight. It seemed the ability to create new artworks at will had returned.

In 2019, the trial or working exhibition of the growing number of artworks found a site in a large dairy factory at Pihama in Coastal Taranaki now repurposed for events and displays, and a boutique lavender oil enterprise. By May 2021, the exhibition *Songs of the Earth (1972 – 2021)* was installed and open to view. The Installation represented the culmination of fifty years of artistic endeavour and discovery while, similarly, the twenty-year Shakespeare/Duchamp publication project under the Quaternary Institute was coming to a natural conclusion.

The successful completion of an artistic project spanning fifty years and the intervening determination of the basis of Duchamp's seminal creativity centred on his *Bride Stripped bare by Her Bachelors, Even* aka *Large Glass* was followed by cracking the mystery around Shakespeare's legendary oeuvre by appreciating the *Sonnet* philosophy. Both projects pivot on the nature-based female/male-validating philosophy germane to all human beings as their birthright philosophy.

The sentiments expressed in the two notes of 1972 written at the beginning of the new realisation of purpose and creativity have now been vindicated and enhanced immeasurably by a nature-based philosophy that back then was a mere intuition. The completed Installation *Songs of the Earth (1972 – 2021)* and the nine published volumes speak amply in response to those early murmurings.

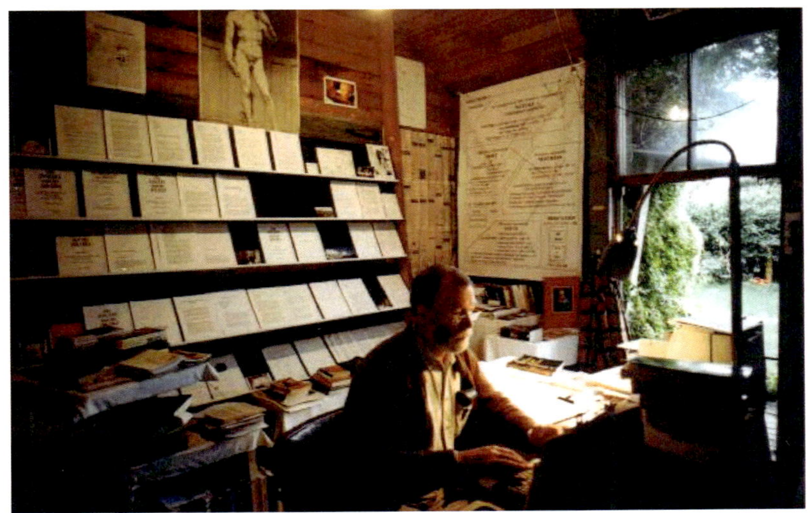

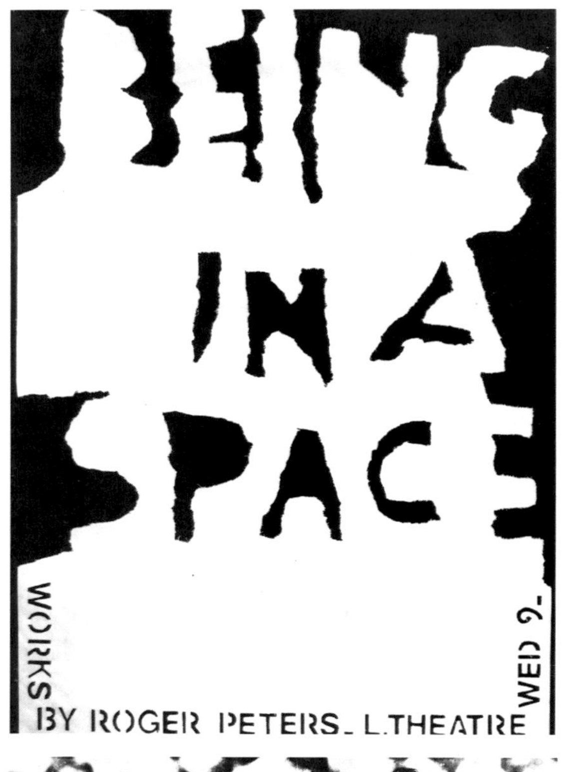


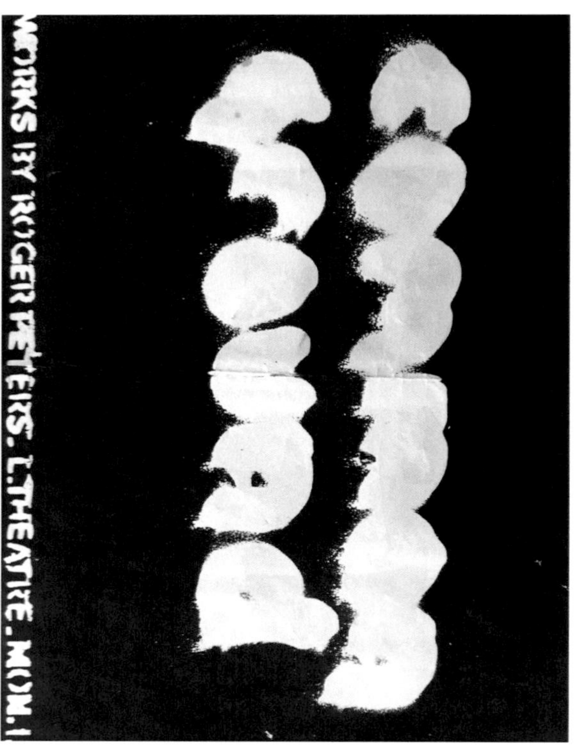

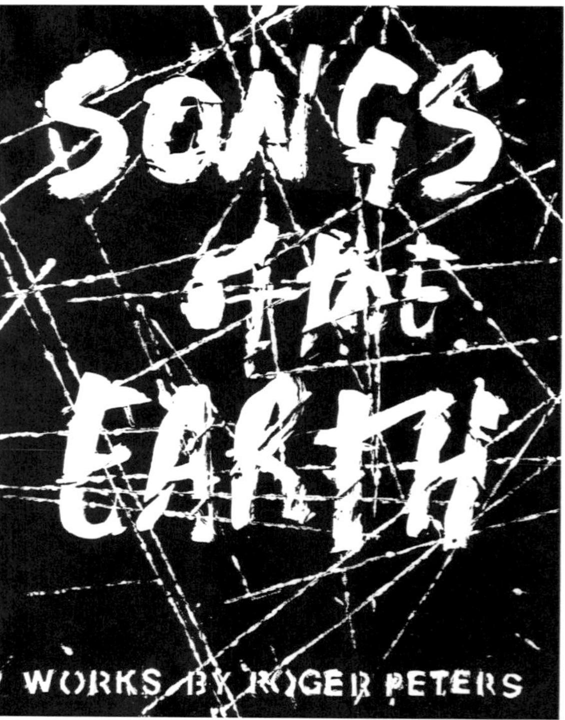


## POSTERS - 1972-1975

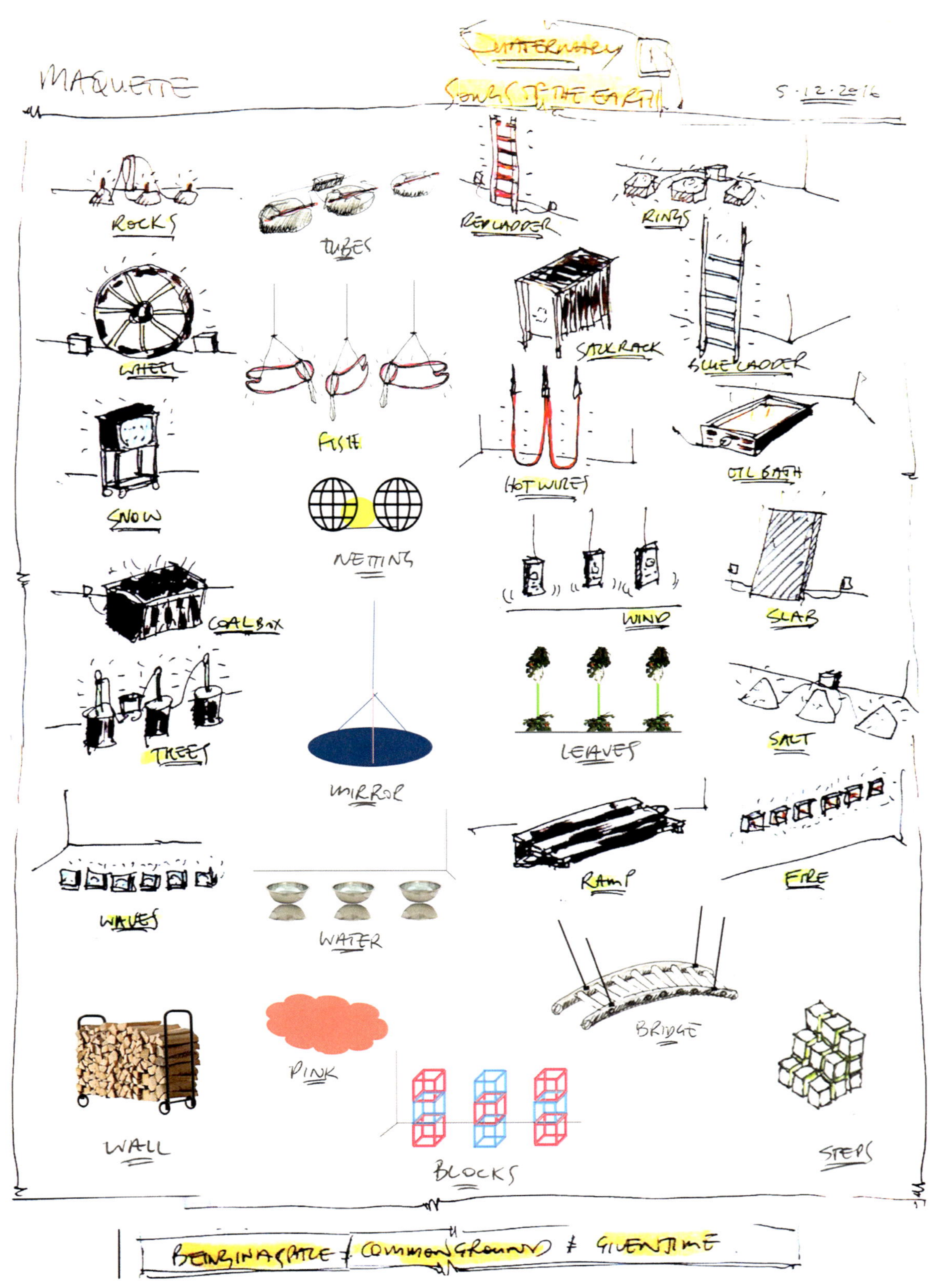

MAQUETTE
Songs of the Earth
5·12·2016
ROCKS
TUBES
RED LADDER
RINGS
WHEEL
SACK RACK
BLUE LADDER
FISH
SNOW
HOT WIRES
OIL BATH
NETTING
WIND
SLAB
COAL BOX
TREES
MIRROR
LEAVES
SALT
WAVES
RAMP
FIRE
WATER
PINK
BRIDGE
WALL
BLOCKS
STEPS
BEING IN A PLACE + COMMON GROUND + GIVEN TIME

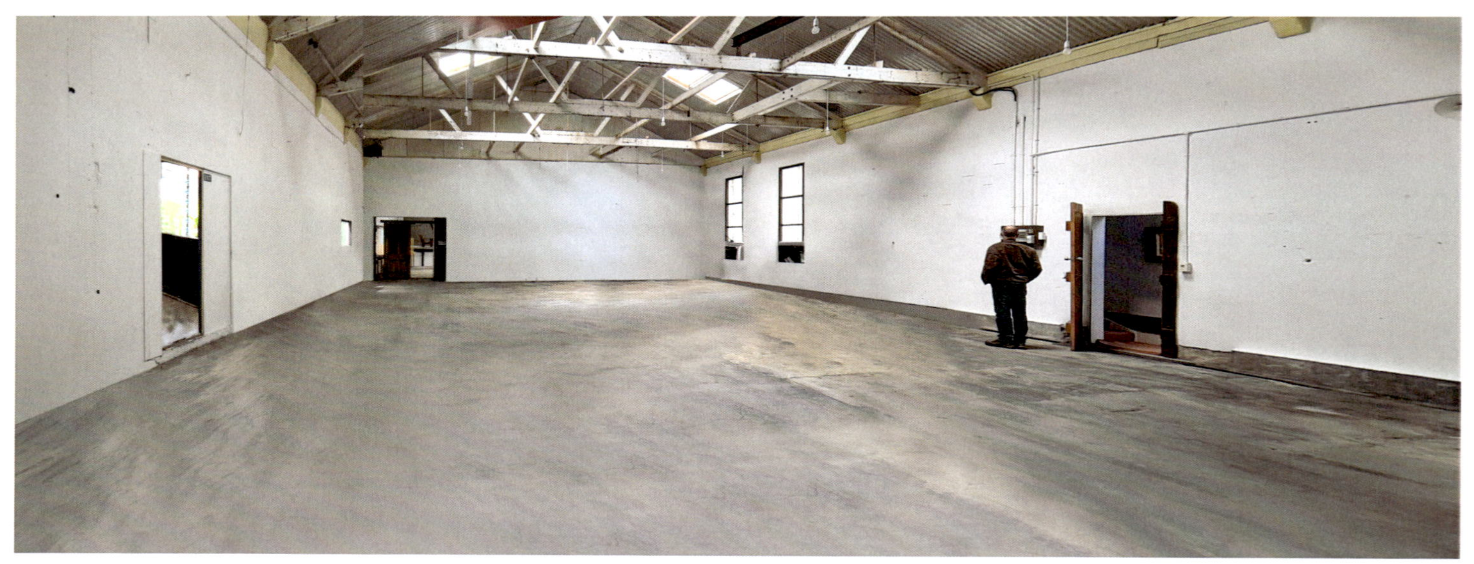

PIHAMA LAVENDER - EXHIBITION SPACE
Coastal Taranaki, NZ

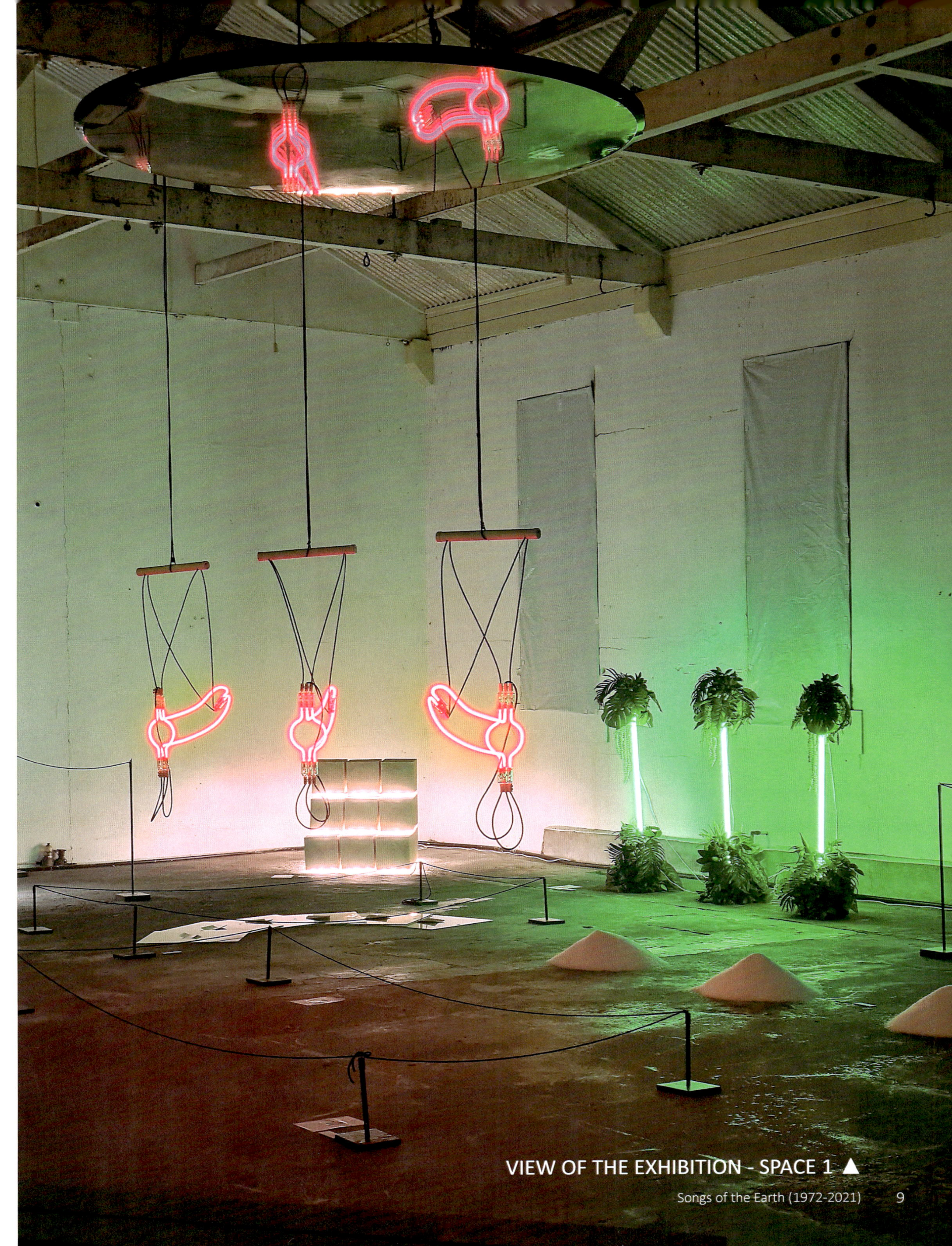


VIEW OF THE EXHIBITION - SPACE 1 ▲
Songs of the Earth (1972-2021)    9

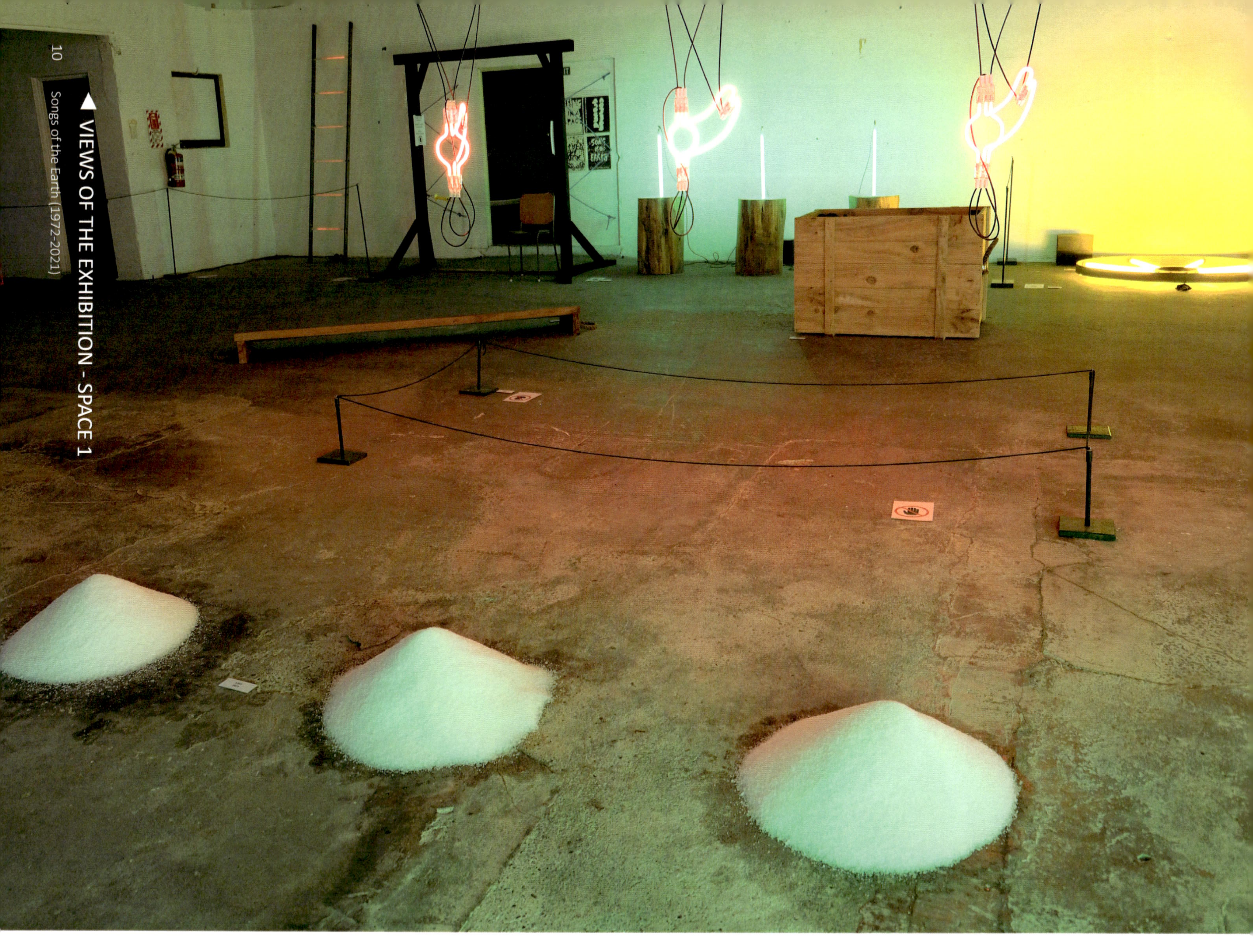

▲ VIEWS OF THE EXHIBITION - SPACE 1

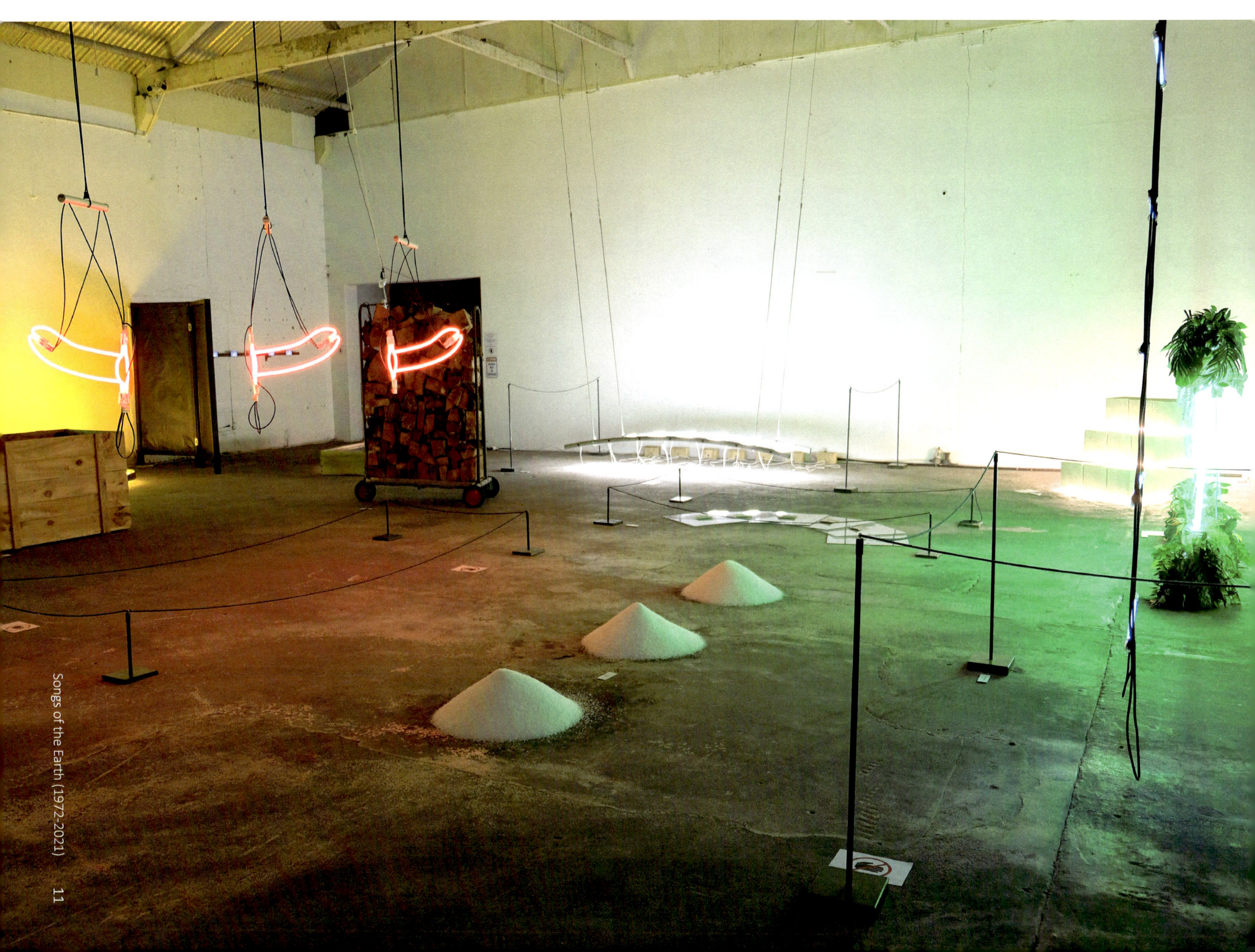

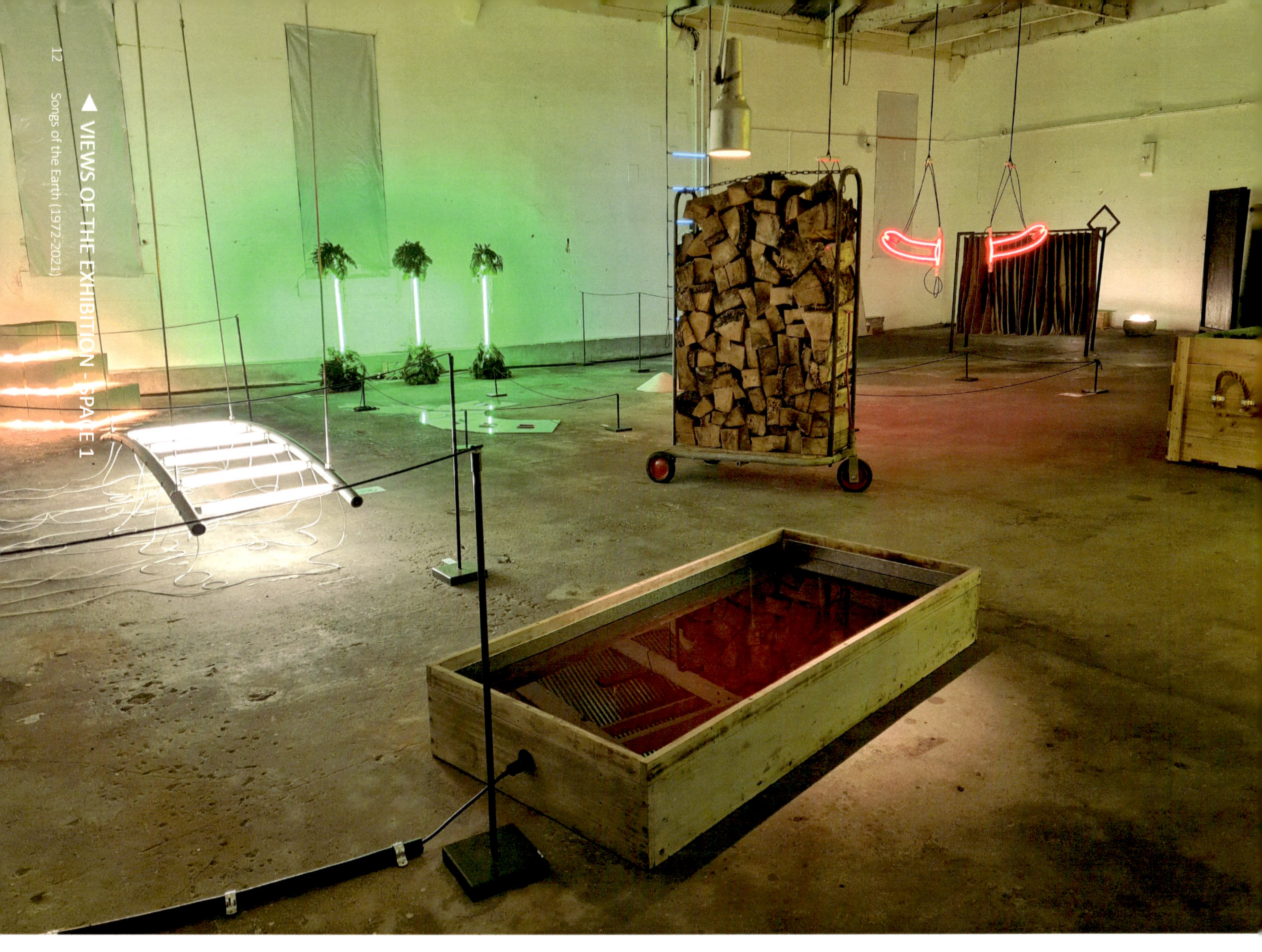



 Songs of the Earth (1972-2021)

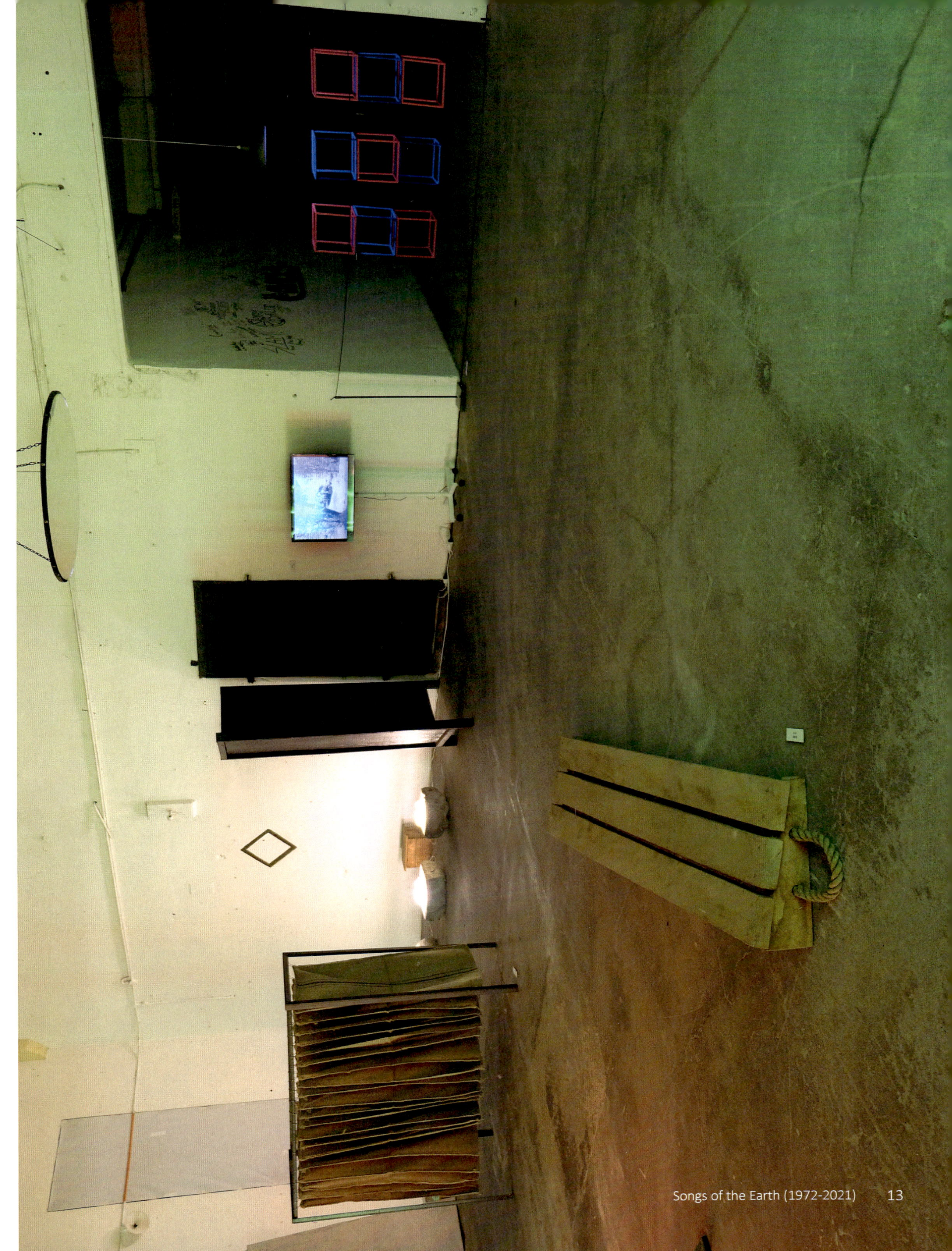

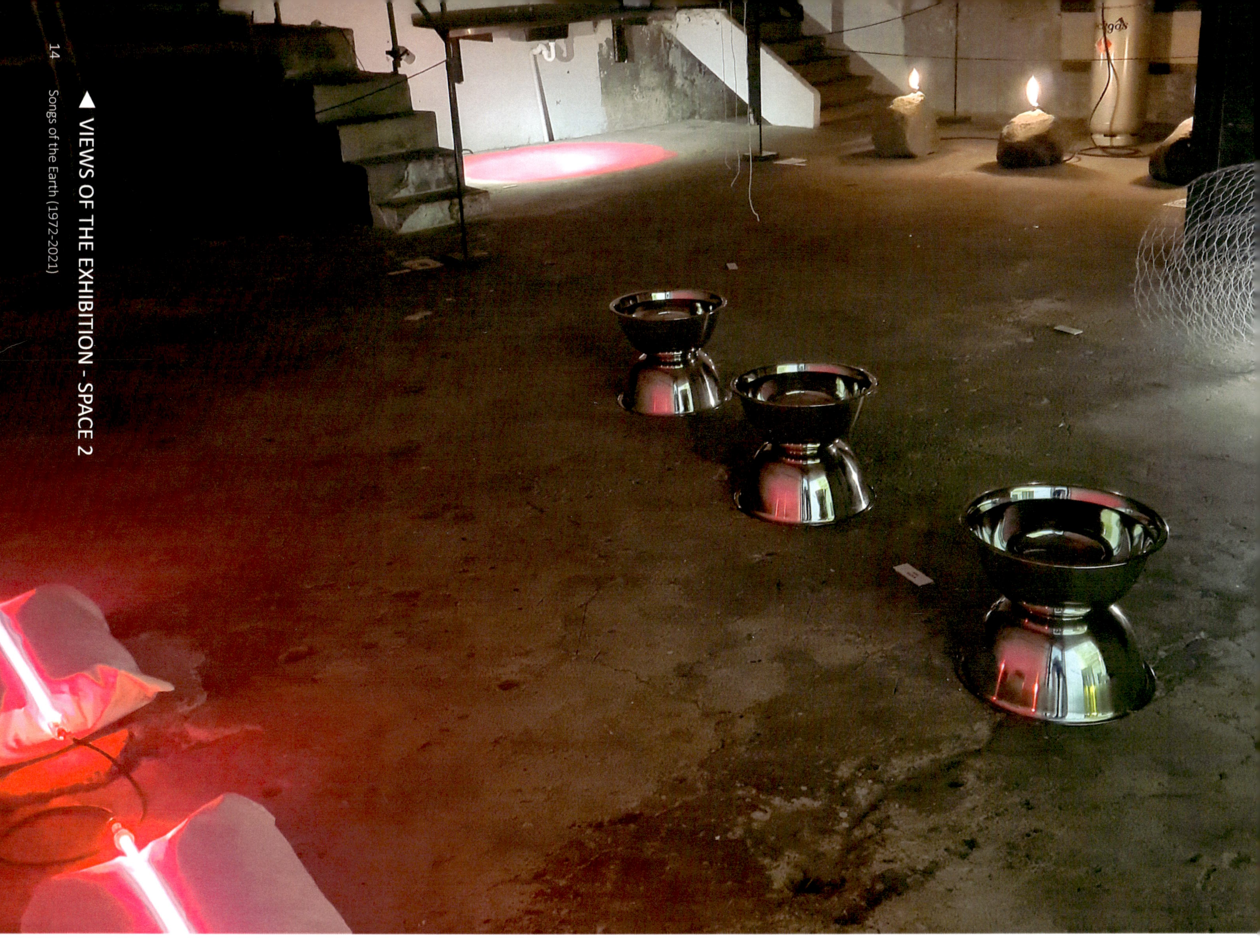



▲ VIEWS OF THE EXHIBITION - SPACE 2

Songs of the Earth (1972-2021)

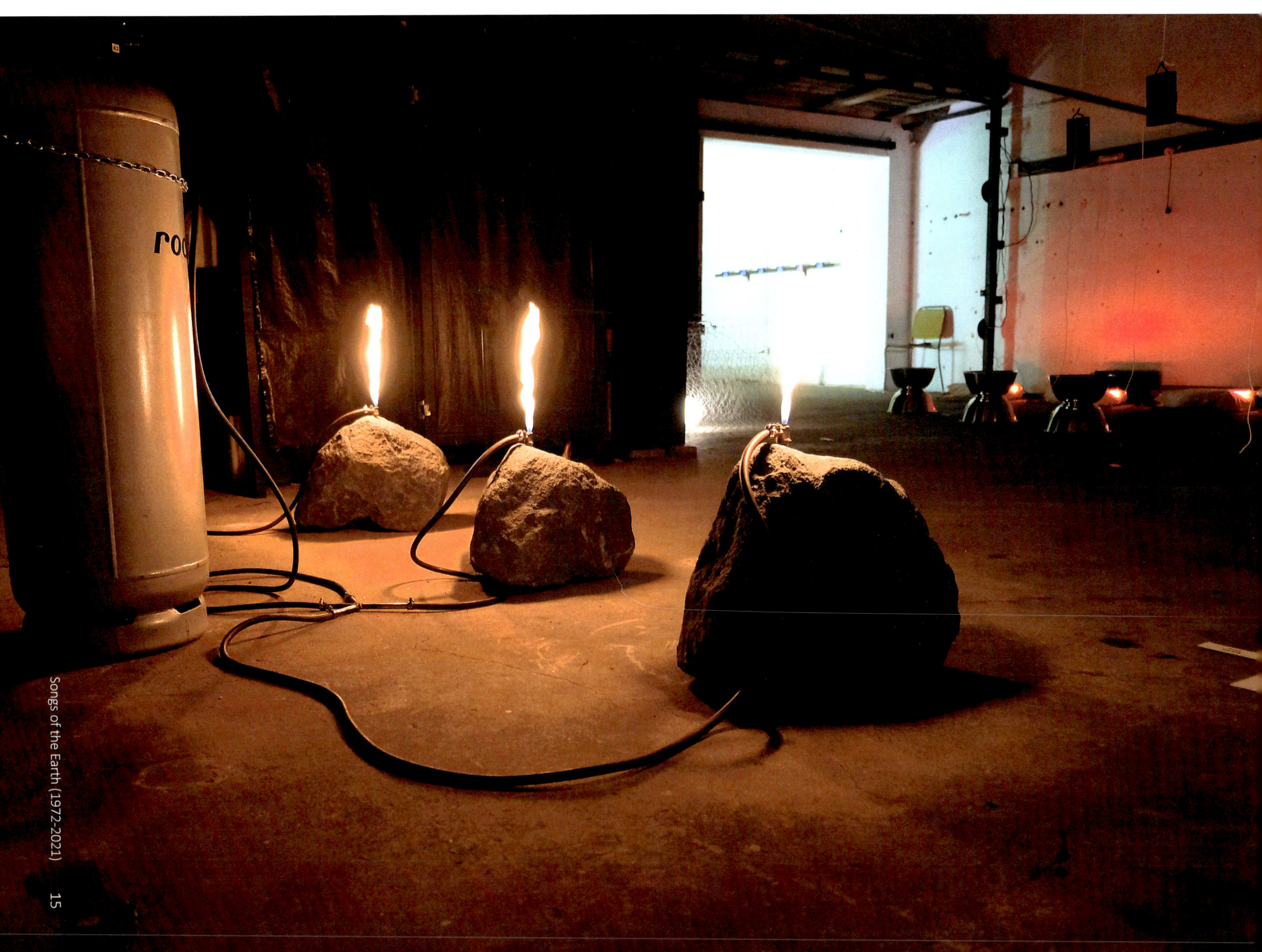

# INDIVIDUAL WORKS

| TITLE | MATERIAL & SIZE: height x width x depth |
| --- | --- |
| RED LADDER 1972 | heater elements; screws; ceramic insulators;<br>steel uprights; wiring<br>2600 x 620 x 200 mm |
| RAMP 1972 | timber; nails; rope<br>200 x 2500 x 500 mm |
| SNOW 1973 (2020) | flat screen TV; USB stick;<br>steel stand; castor wheels<br>1300 x 760 x 350 mm |
| SALT 1973 | sea salt<br>250 x 2200 x 600 mm |
| SACK RACK 1972 | sacks; stainless hooks; steel frame<br>1500 x 1680 x 770 mm |
| RINGS 1975 | limestone blocks; circular fluorescent tubes;<br>brass stanchions; wiring; wooden box<br>200 x 2100 x 430 mm |
| COAL BOX 1972 | timber; nails; coal; rope<br>770 x 1300 x 750 mm |
| LEAVES 2019 | green fluorescent tubes; wiring;<br>artificial leaves and flowers; concrete pavers;<br>wiring; chokes and starters; wooden box<br>1450 x 2000 x 400 mm |
| WALL 2020 | steel and wooden trolley; rubber wheels;<br>galvanised pipe; steel chain; split fire wood<br>1720 x 1300 x 720 mm |
| OIL BATH 1972 | timber; screws; galvanised tray;<br>element; wiring; heated transformer oil to 36°C<br>260 x 1780 x 820 mm |
| STEPS 2018 | plywood boxes; sand and paint;<br>LED light bulbs; sockets; wiring<br>800 x 800 x800 mm |
| BLOCKS 2019 | wooden doweling; fluorescent paint;<br>UV light; lampshade; wiring<br>1000 x 1800 x 320 mm |
| BRIDGE 2019 | white fluorescent tubes; galvanised steel pipe;<br>connectors; screws; wiring;<br>stainless brackets and tubes; turnbuckles;<br>steel wire; screw eyes<br>400 x 2660 x 550 mm |
| WAVES 1973 (2020) | polaroid photographs; glass panels<br>10 x 1800 x 800 mm |

SLAB 1974

concrete; steel mesh; thermostat; wiring;
underfloor heating (body temperature)
2000 x 770 x 250 mm

BLUE LADDER 1974

blue neon tubing; HT cable; brass connectors;
screw eyes; transformer; wooden box
2500 x 700 x 10 mm

FISH 1978 (2018)

pink neon tubes; HT wiring; plastic tubing;
connectors; transformers
1500 x 2500 x 600 mm

FIRE 1974 (2020)

mobile phones; image of fire; angle iron;
steel brackets; screws
1300 x 2150 x 100 mm

WHEEL 1976

steel rings; yellow fluorescent tubes;
connectors and screws; wiring; chokes and starters;
steel boxes
130 x 1580 x 1580 mm

TREES 1977

tree stumps; green neon tubes; HT cable;
connectors; transformer; wooden box
1320 x 2200 x 650 mm

TUBES 2018

red neon tubes; HT wiring; connectors;
plaster bags; pillow slips; transformer;
wooden box
150 x 2100 x 380 mm

ROCKS 1972

volcanic rocks; brass fittings;
rubber tubing; gas bottle
450 x 2000 x 450 mm

WATER 2020

stainless bowls; water
320 x 1800 x 380 mm

WIND 1973

bluetooth speakers (sound of arctic wind);
microchips; string
1500 x 2100 x 100 mm

HOT WIRES 1973

nichrome wire; copper wire; ceramic insulators;
steel connectors; wiring; arc welder
2500 x 1950 x 60 mm

PINK 1973

PVA glue; pink fluorescent paint
5 x 1500 x 1500 mm

NETTING 1973 (2020)

chicken wire; lighting globe; wiring
650 x 1200 x 1000 mm

MIRROR 2020

circular mirror; steel chain; screw eyes; hooks
2400 x 870 x 870 mm

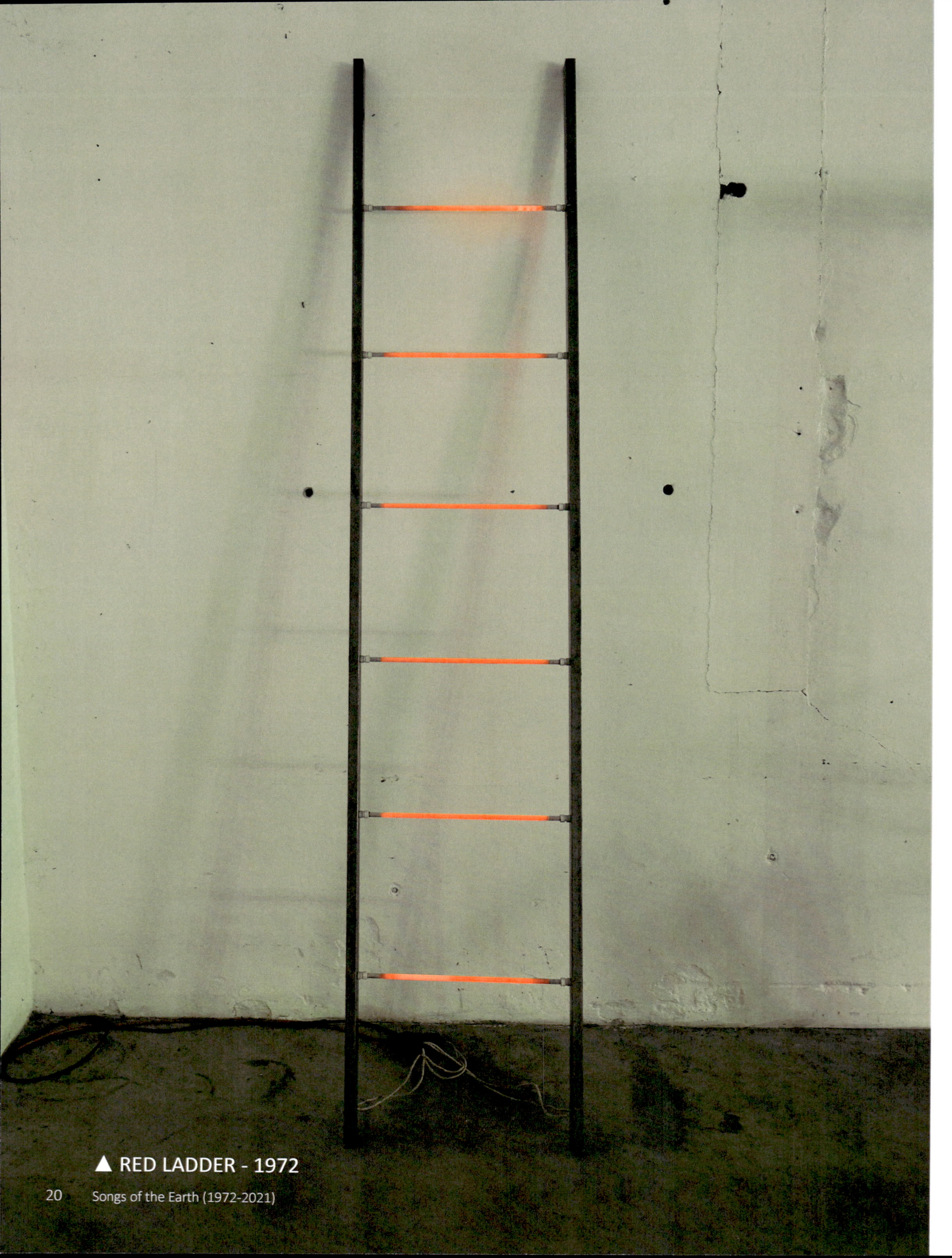


▲ RED LADDER - 1972

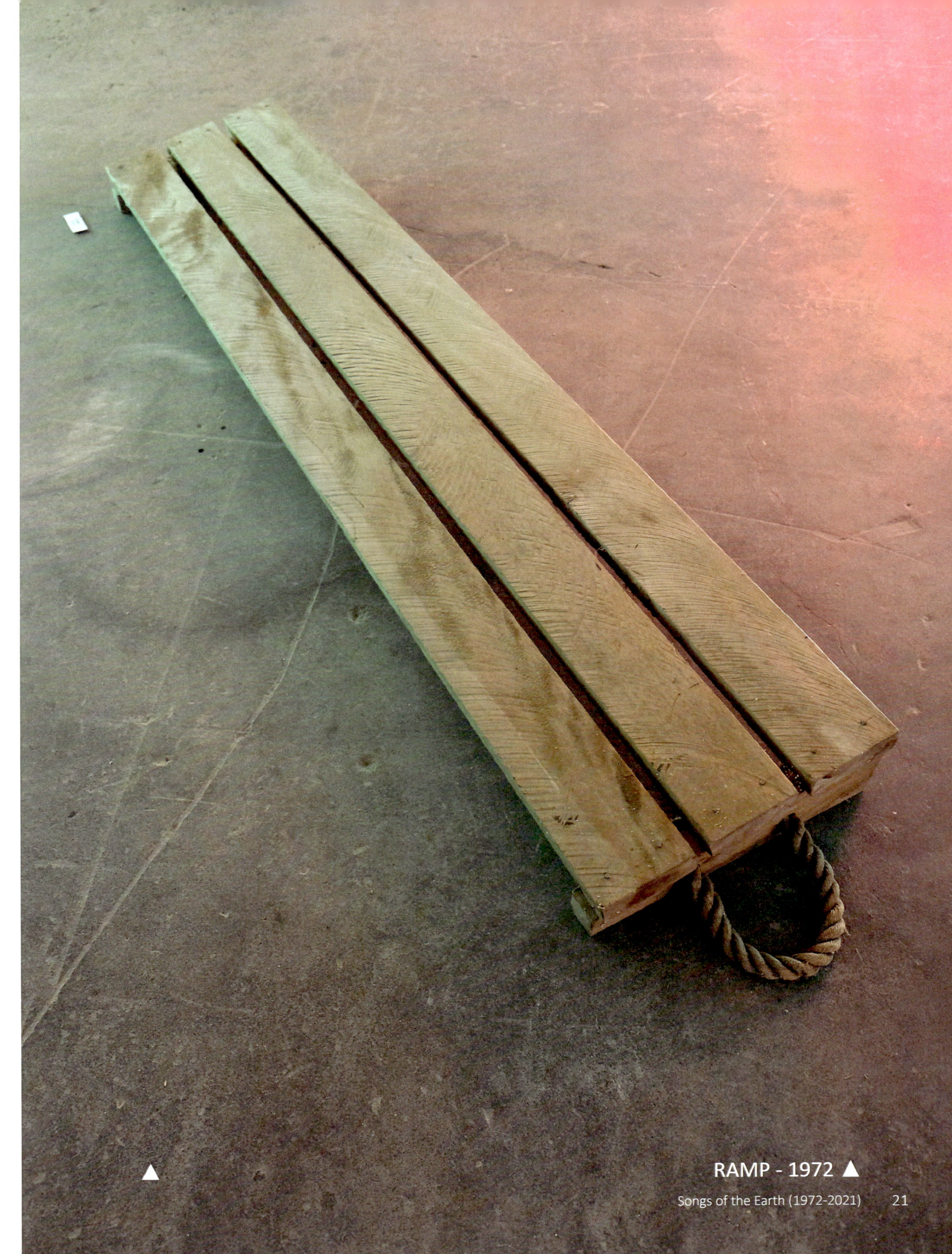



Songs of the Earth (1972-2021)    21

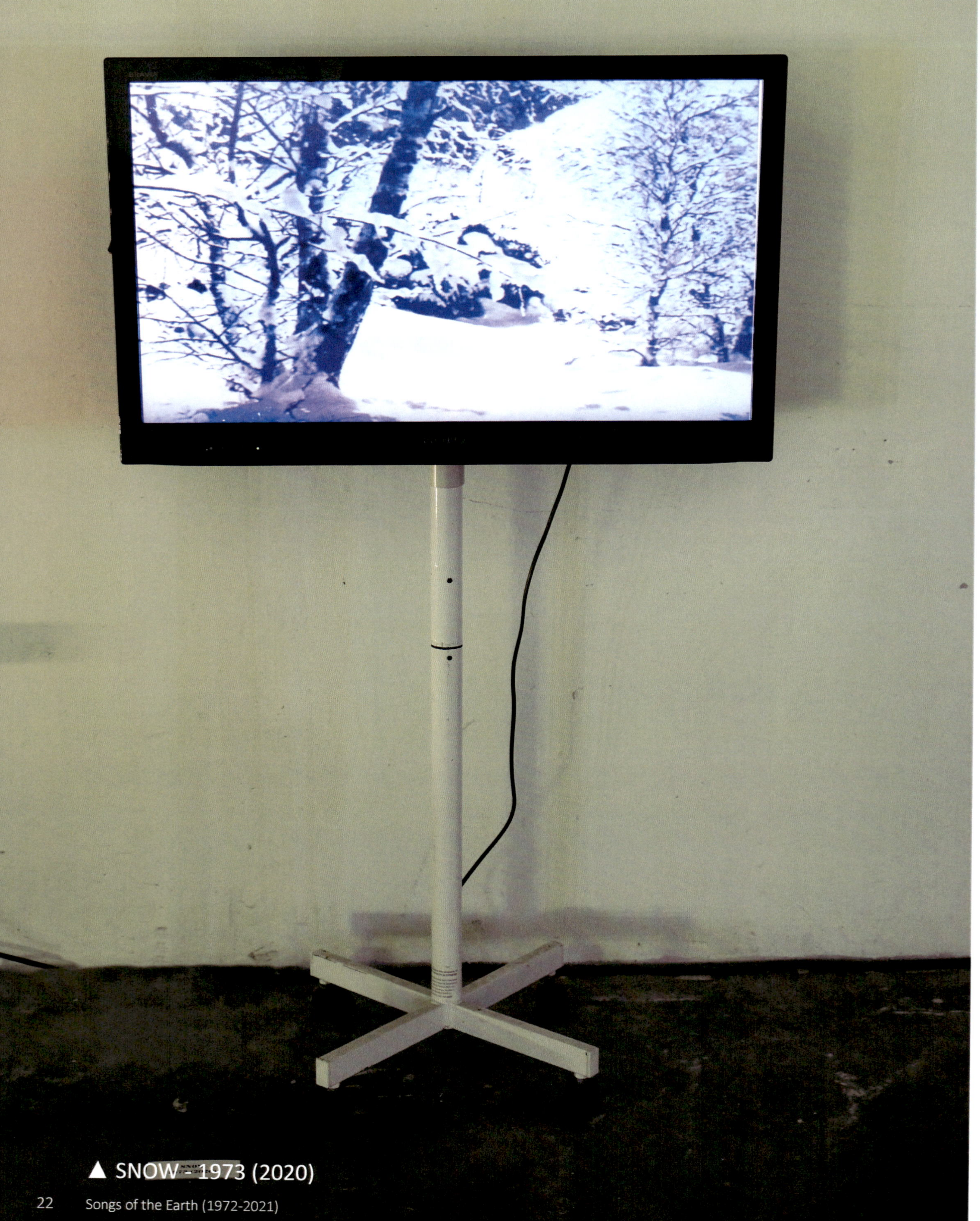



▲ SNOW - 1973 (2020)

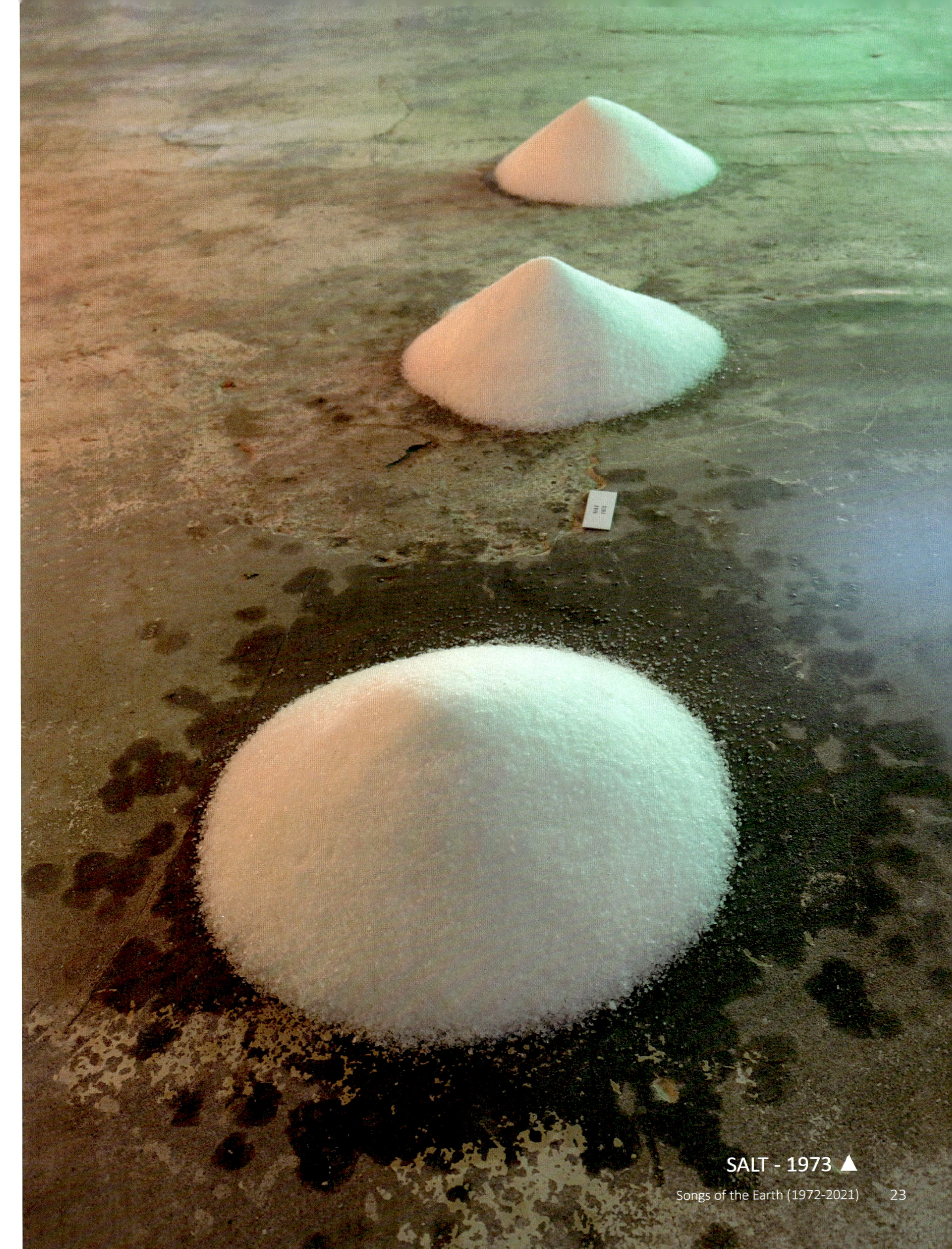



Songs of the Earth (1972-2021)    23

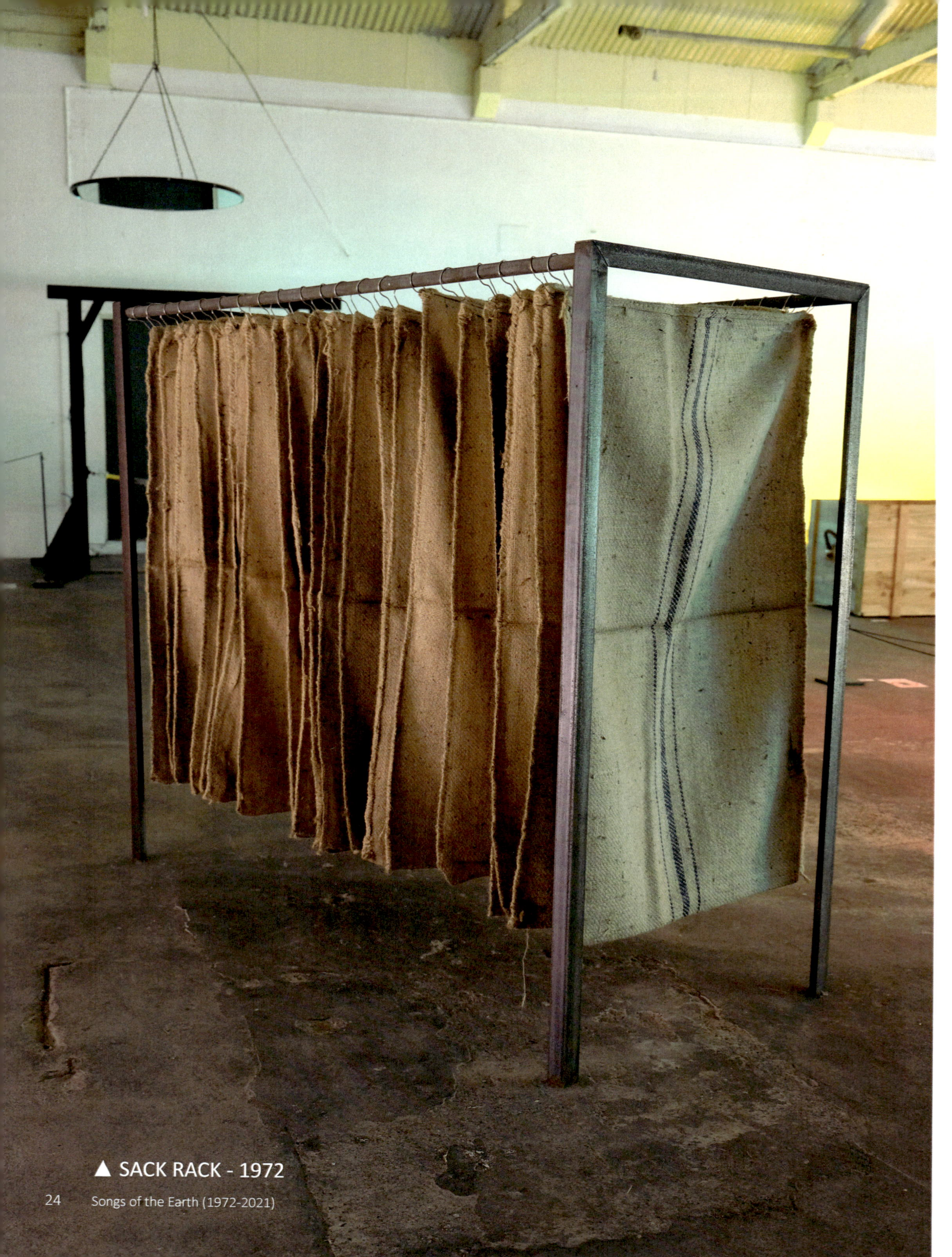


▲ SACK RACK - 1972

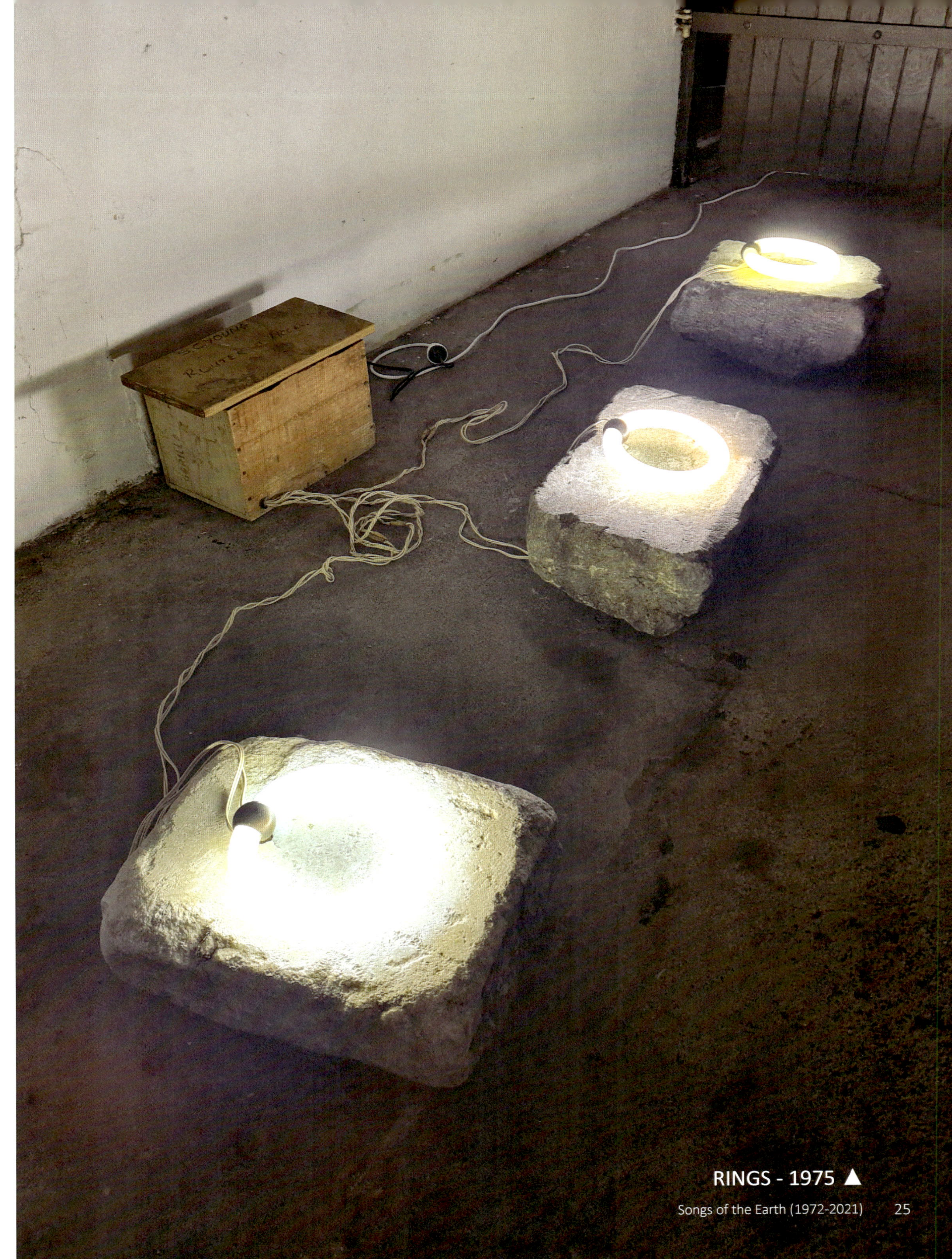



Songs of the Earth (1972-2021)     25

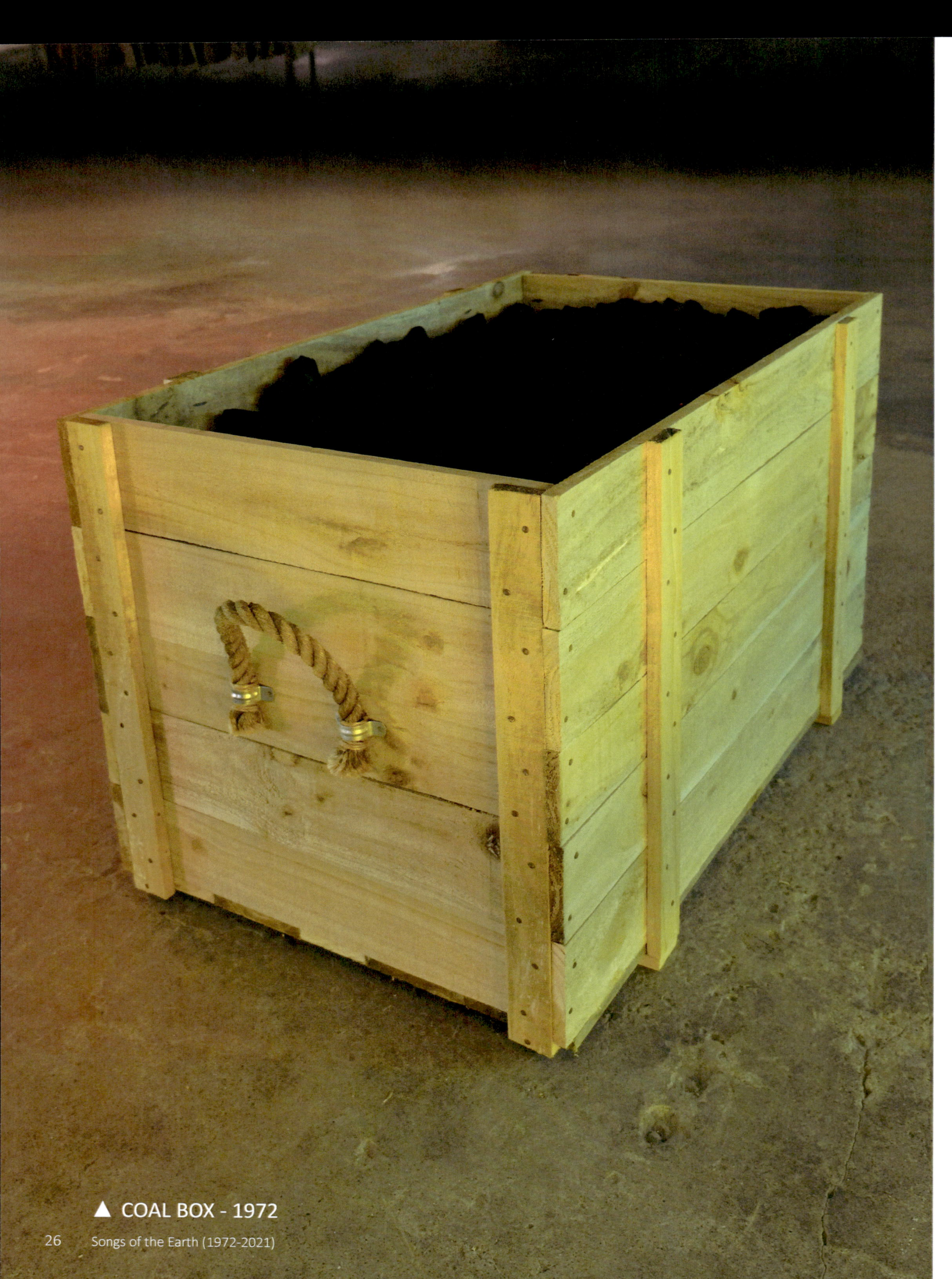

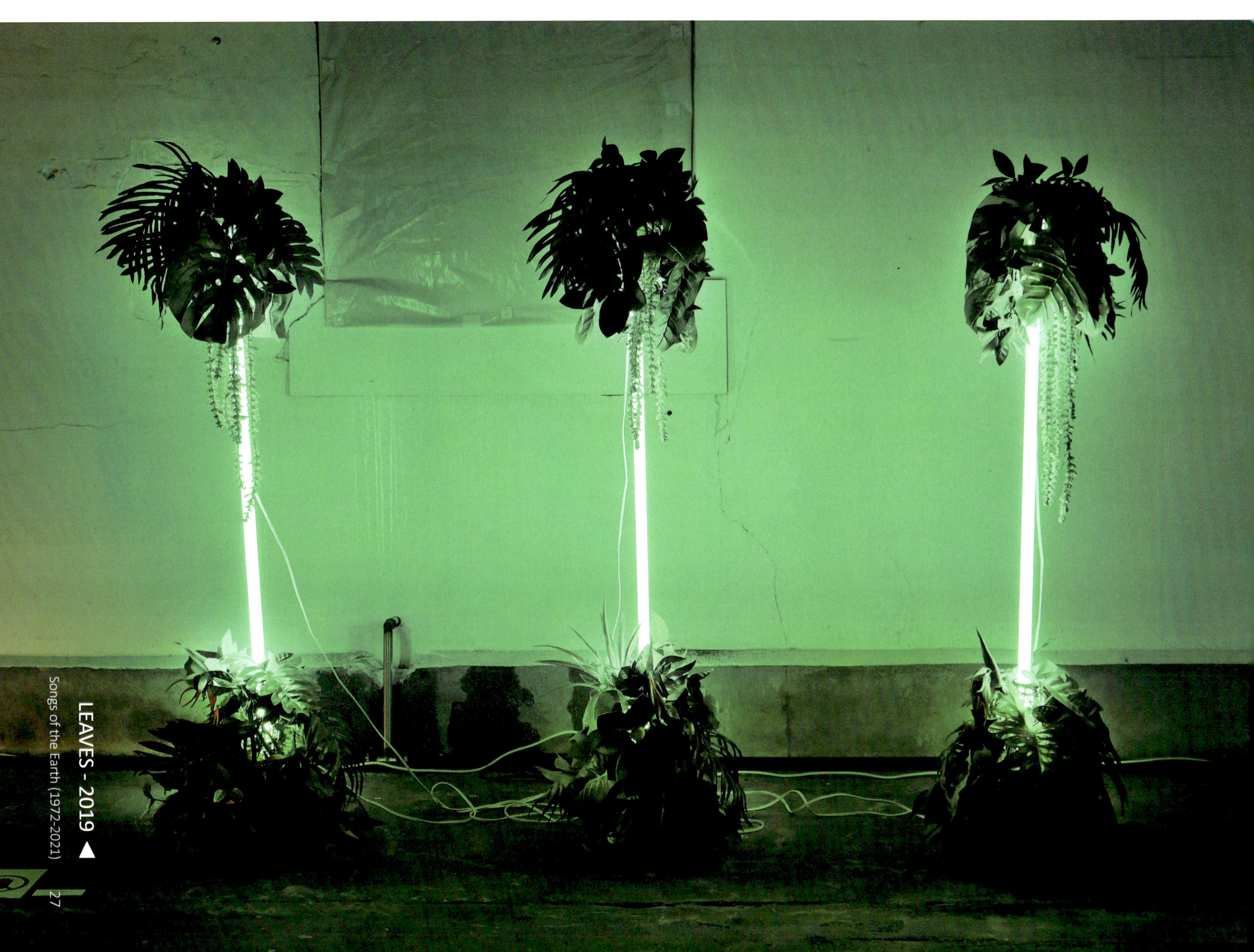

LEAVES - 2019 ▲
Songs of the Earth (1972-2021)    27

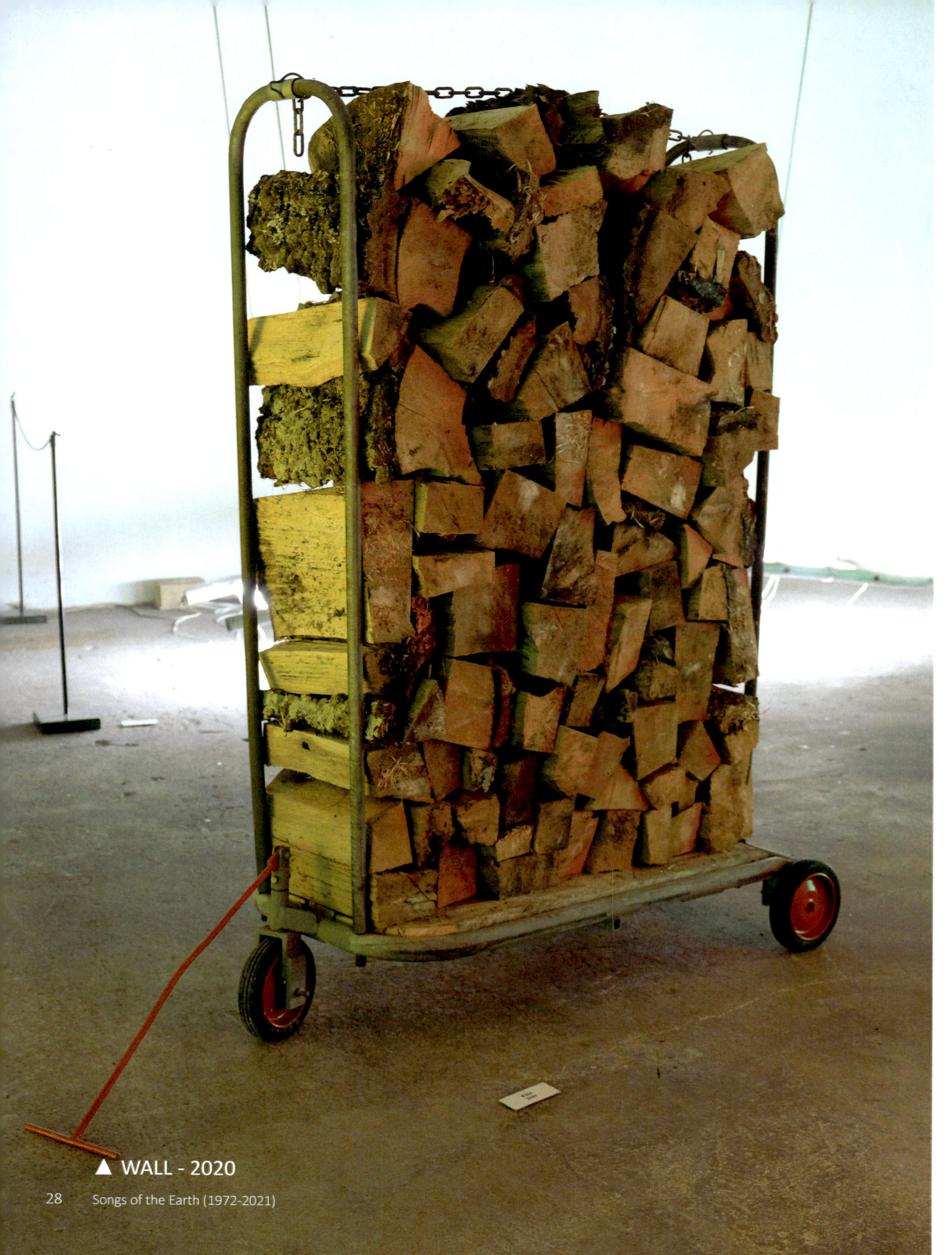

WALL - 2020

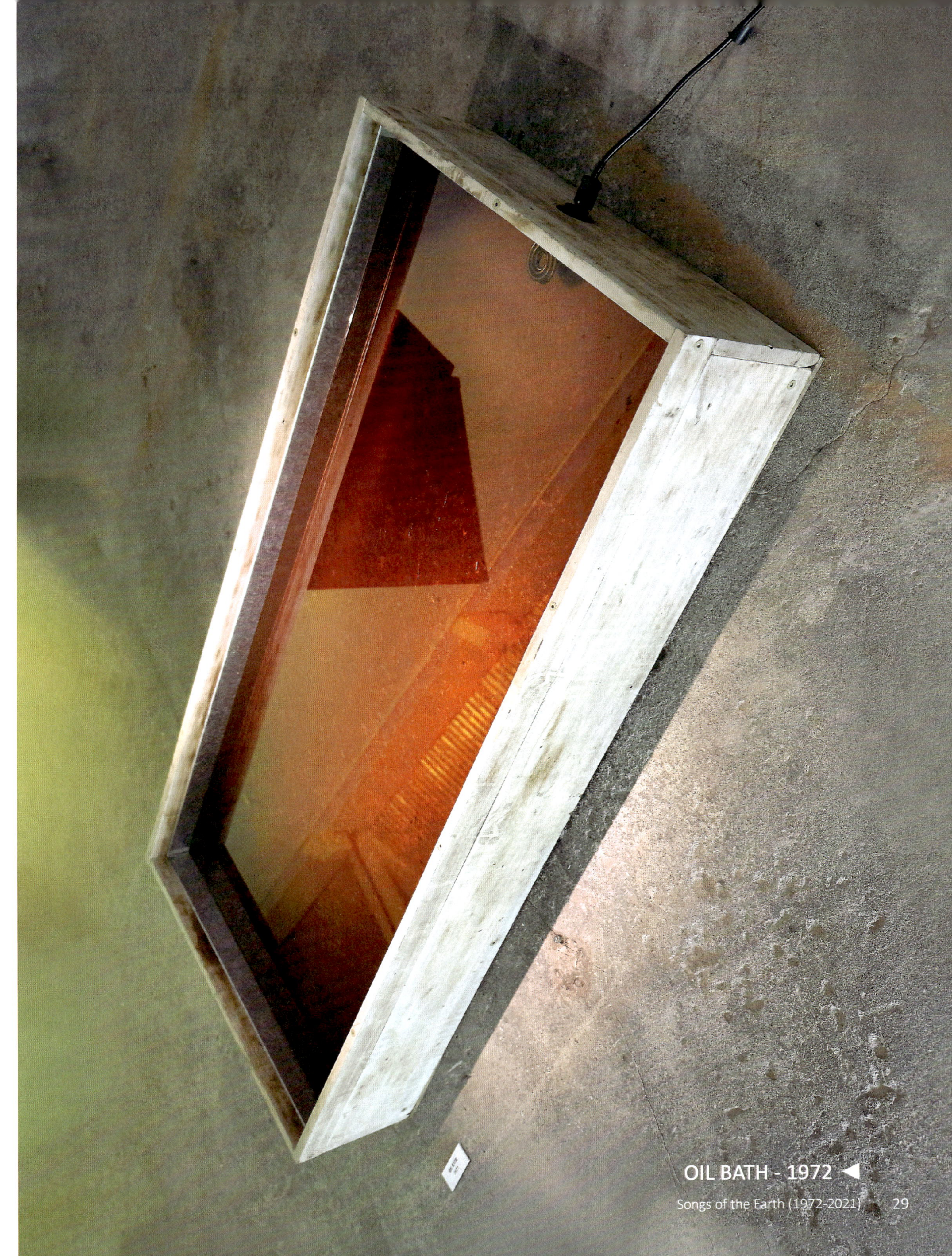


OIL BATH - 1972 ◀

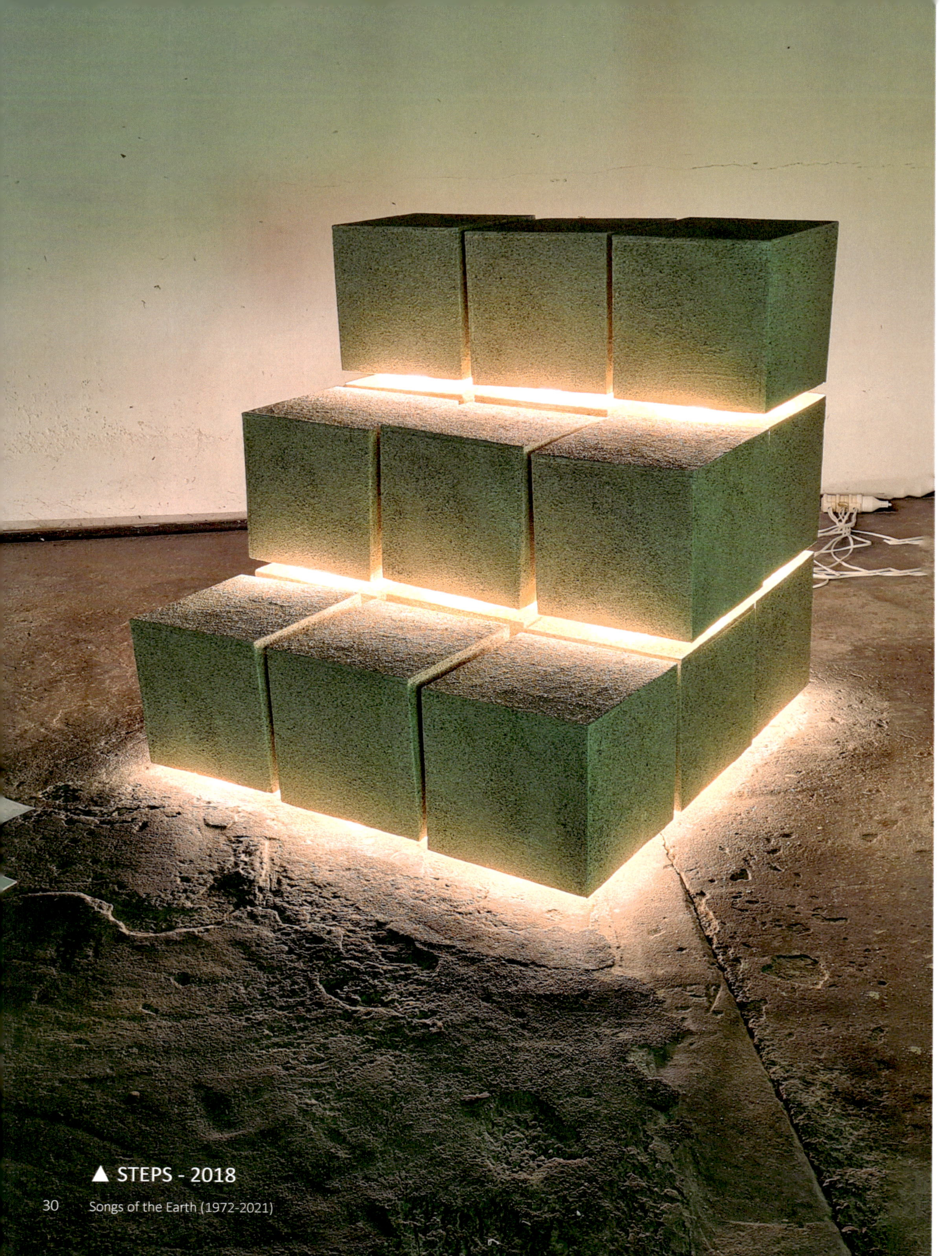


▲ STEPS - 2018

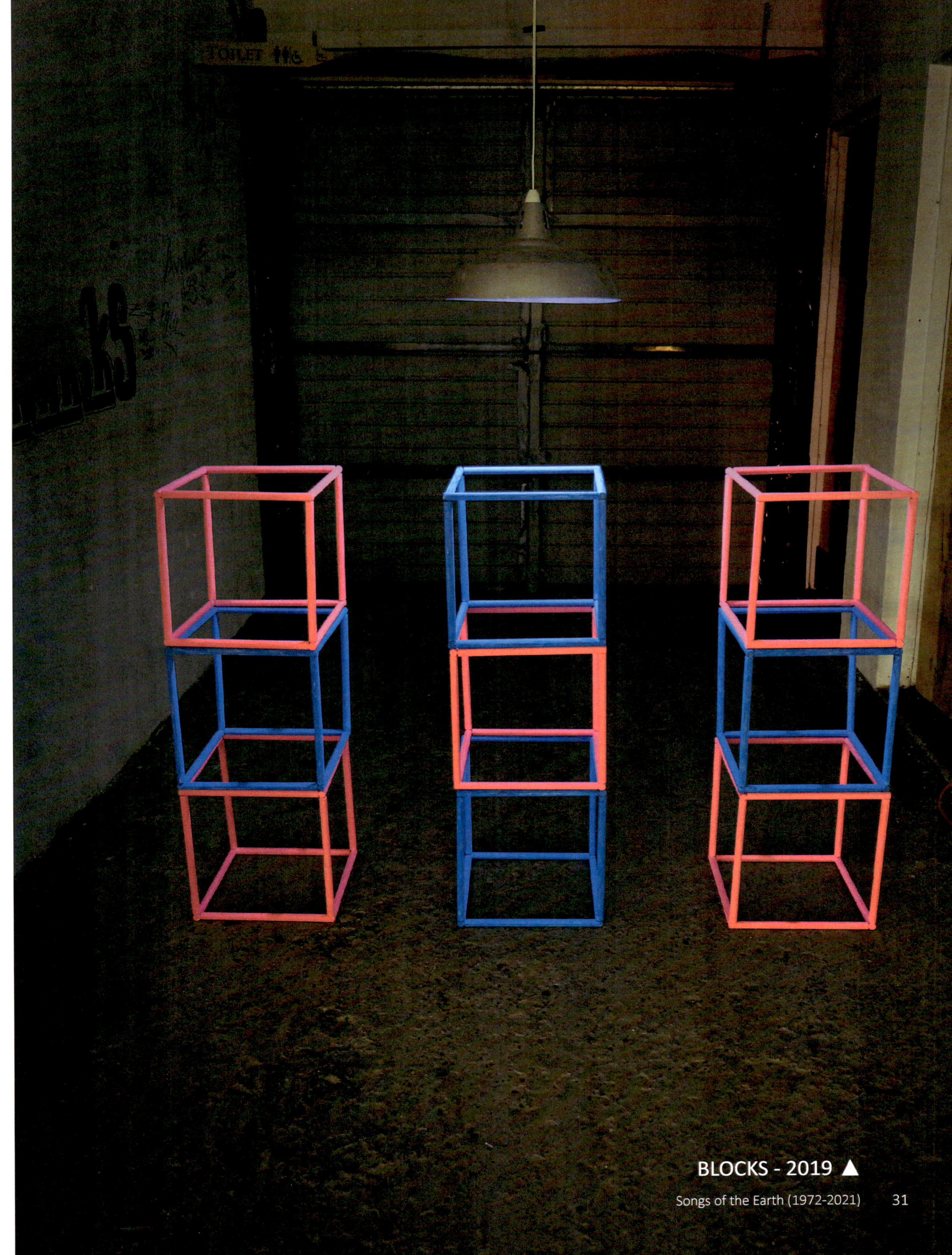

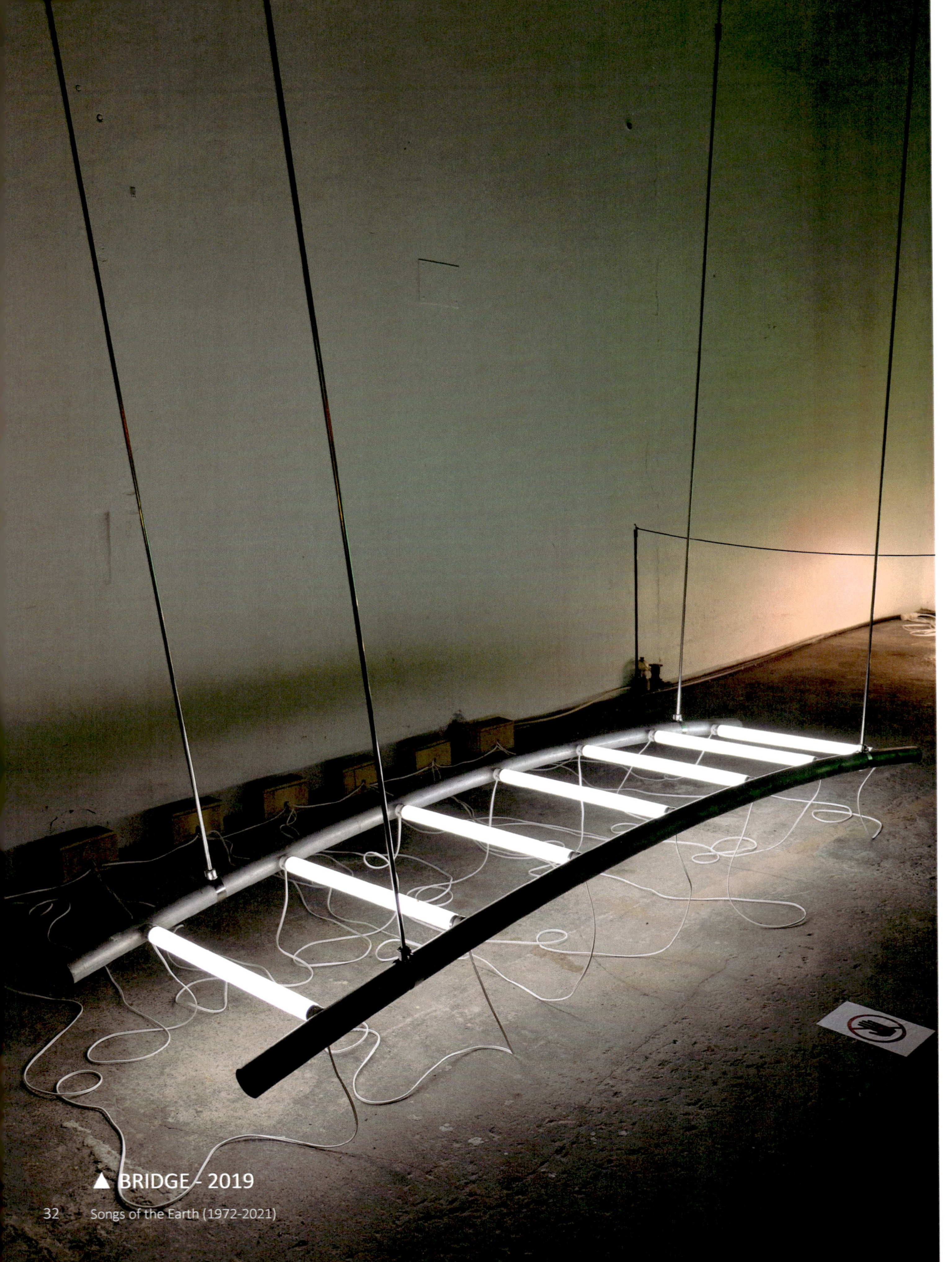

▲ BRIDGE – 2019

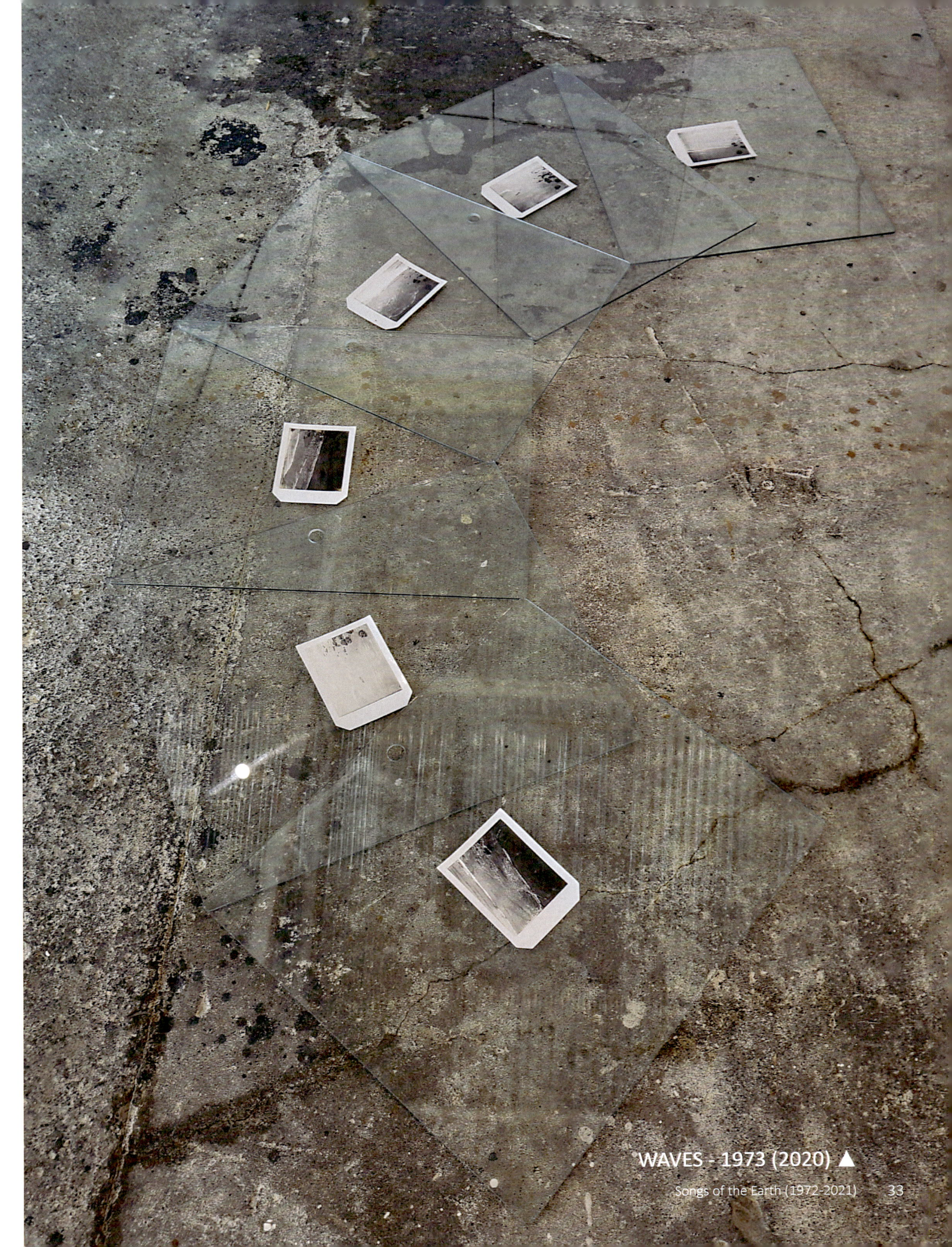

WAVES - 1973 (2020) ▲

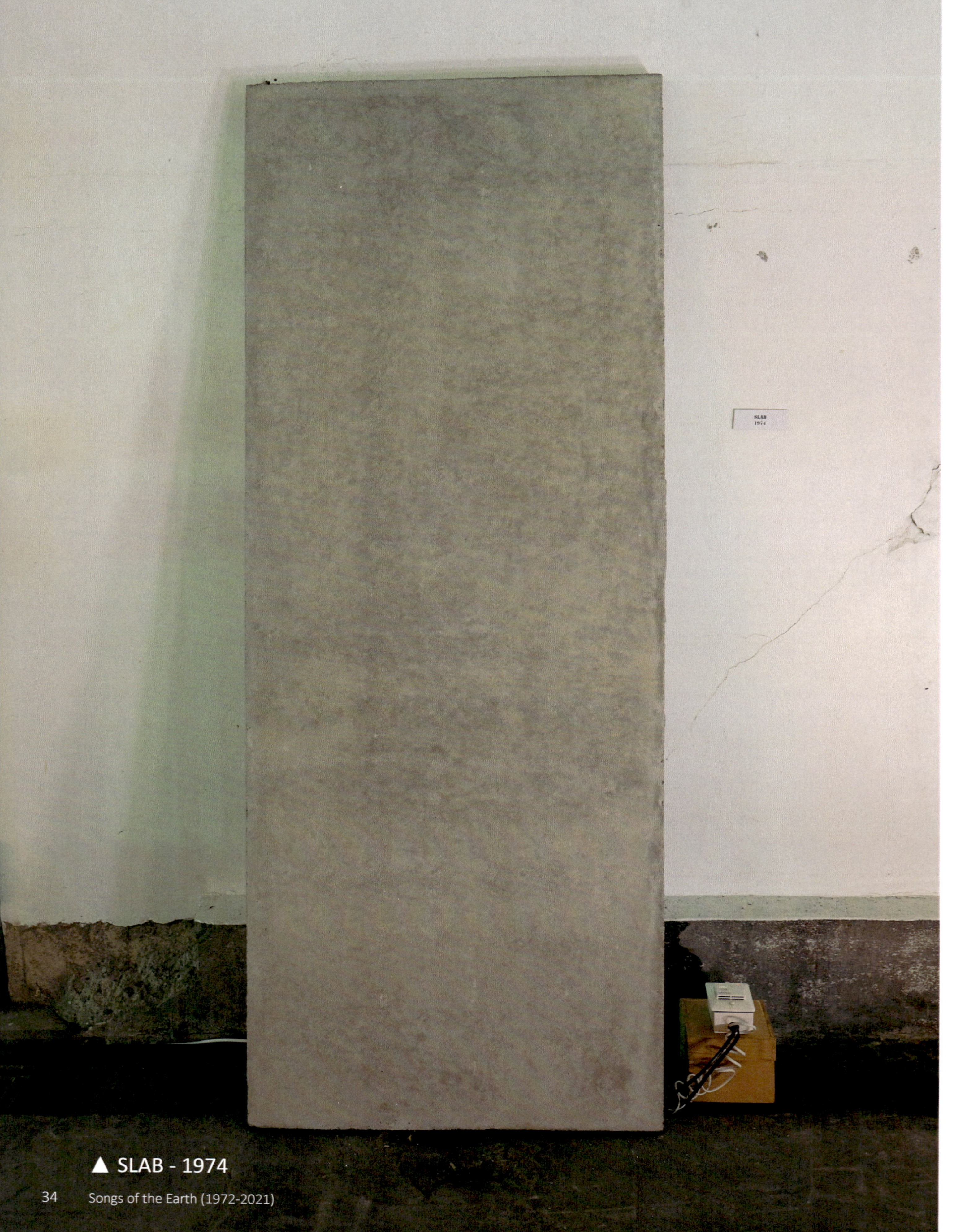


▲ SLAB - 1974

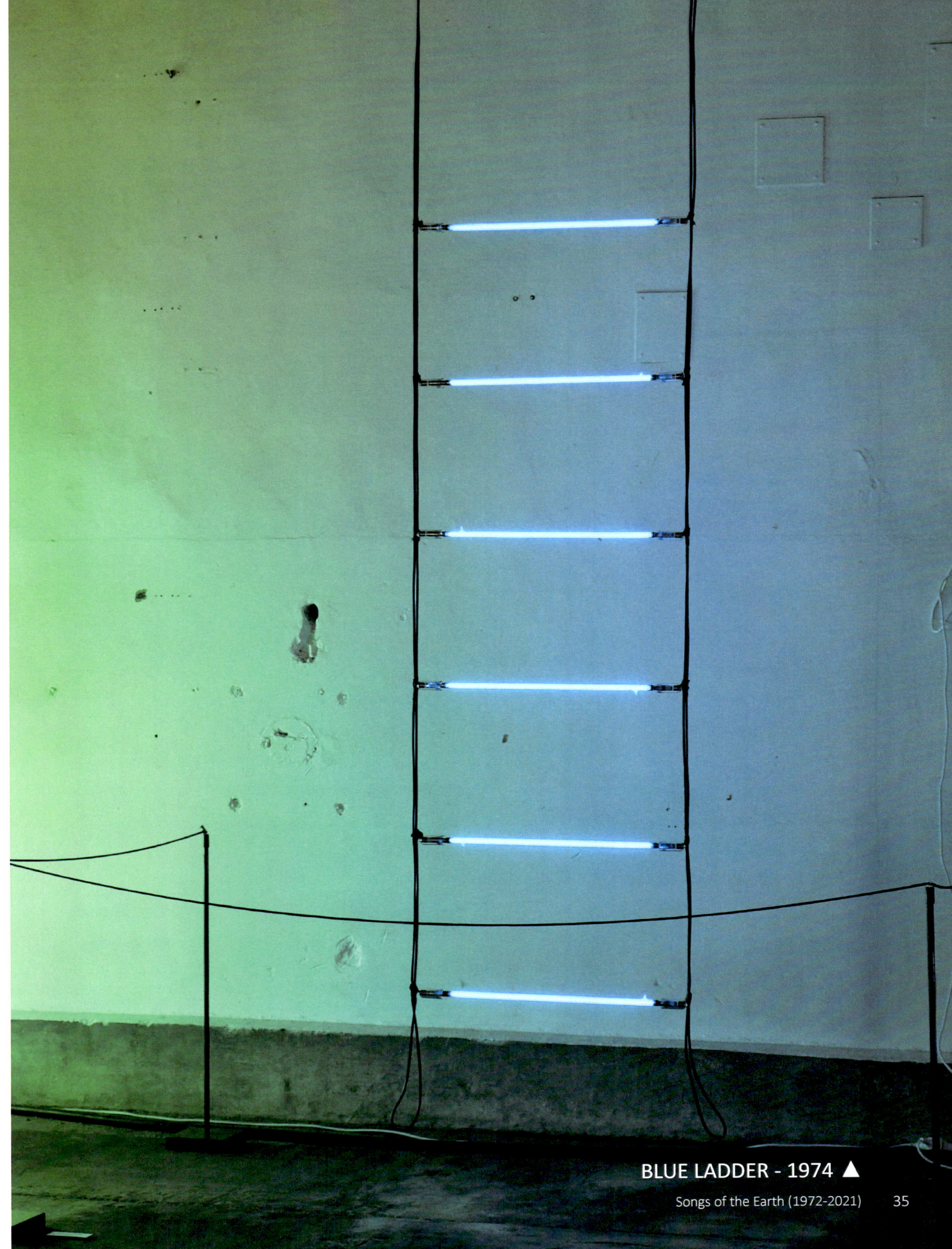

BLUE LADDER - 1974 ▲

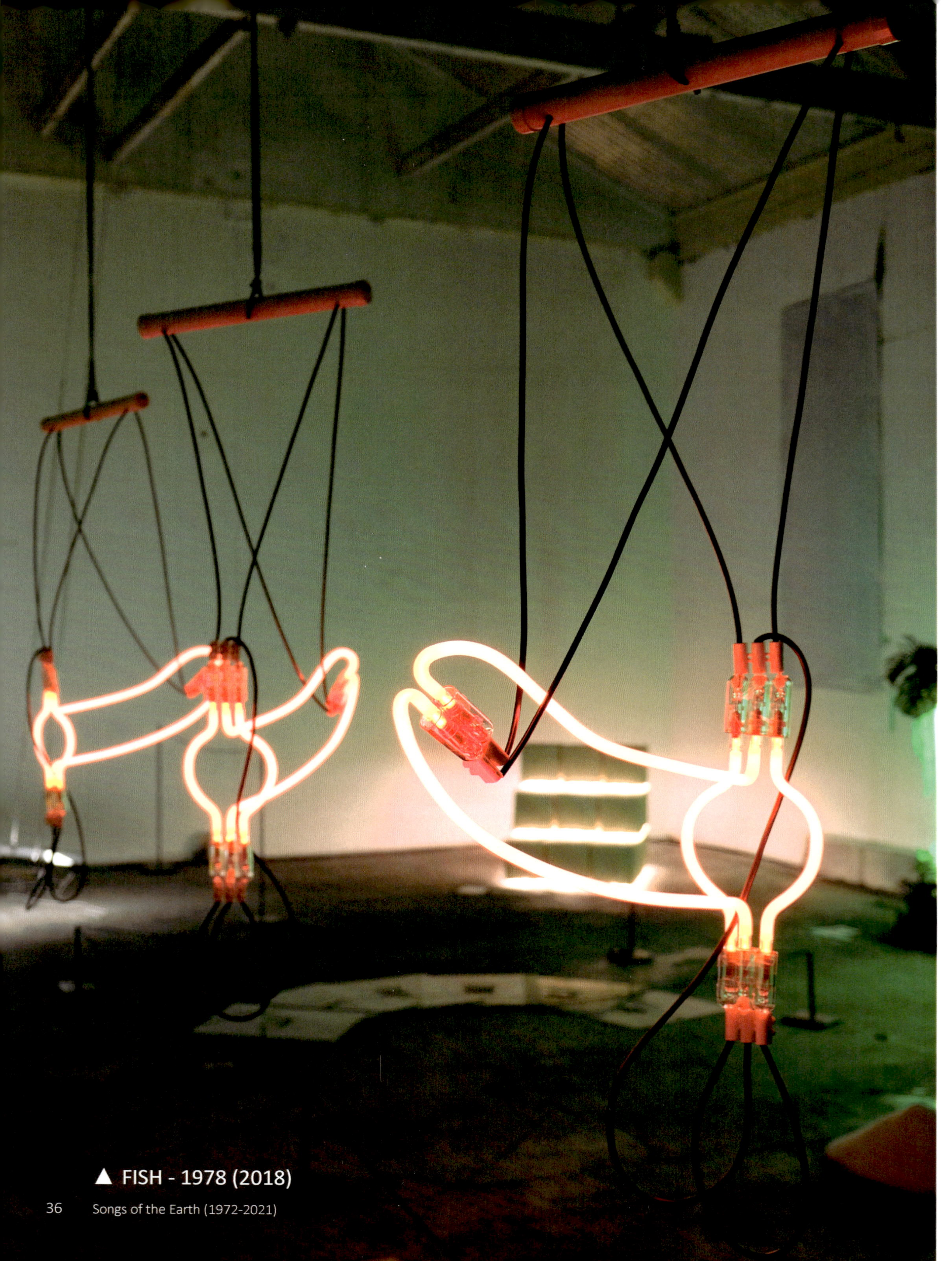

▲ FISH - 1978 (2018)

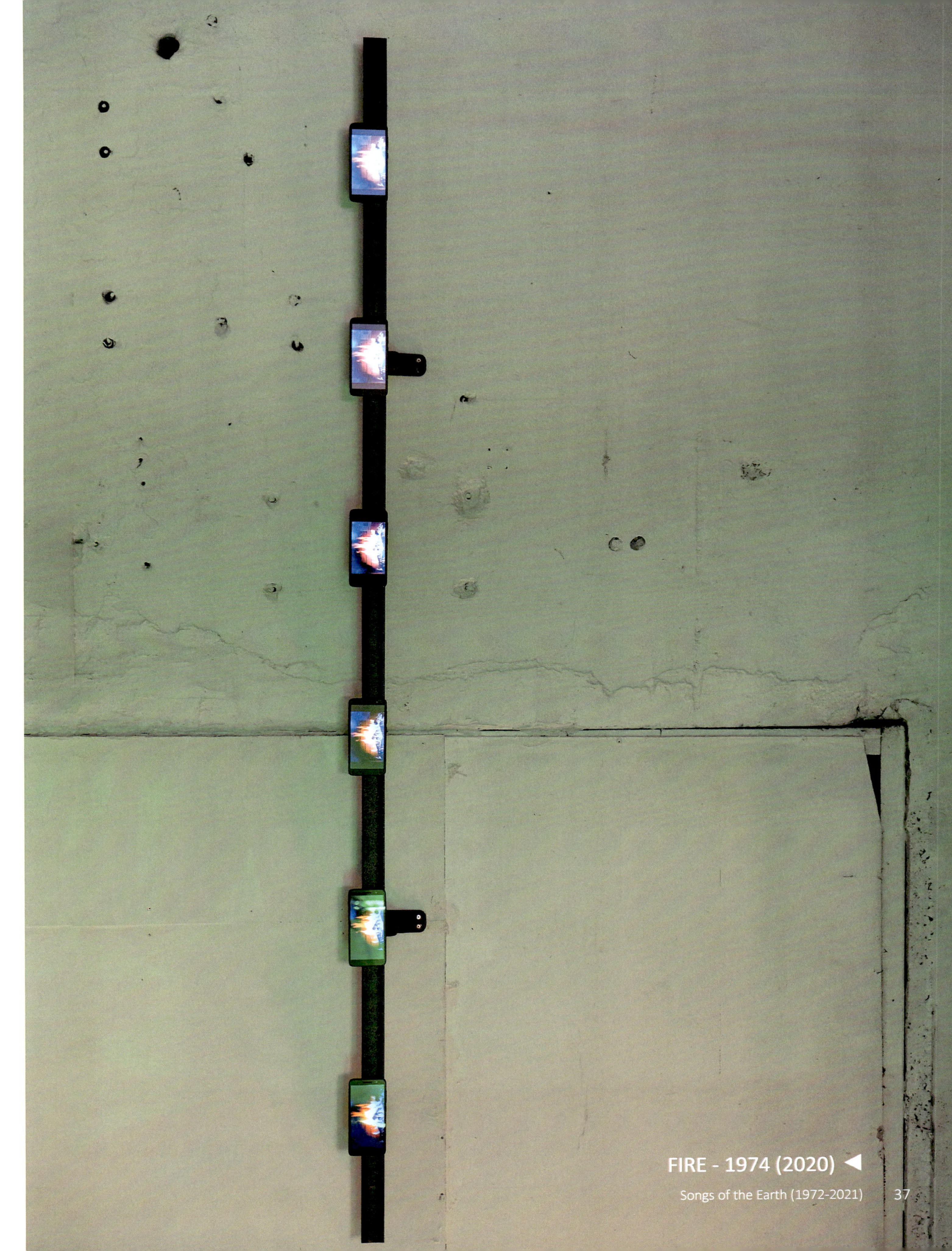

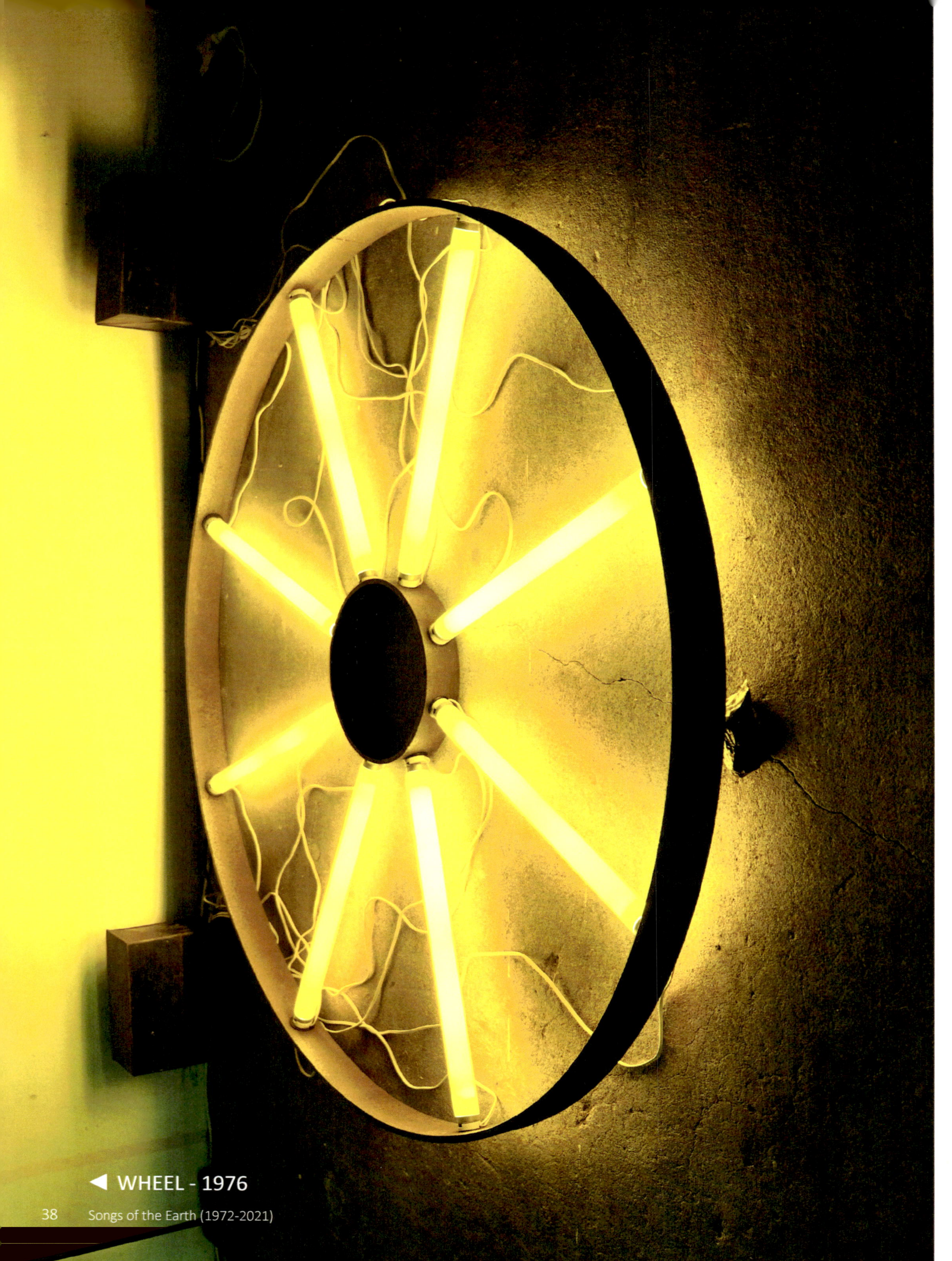

◀ **WHEEL - 1976**

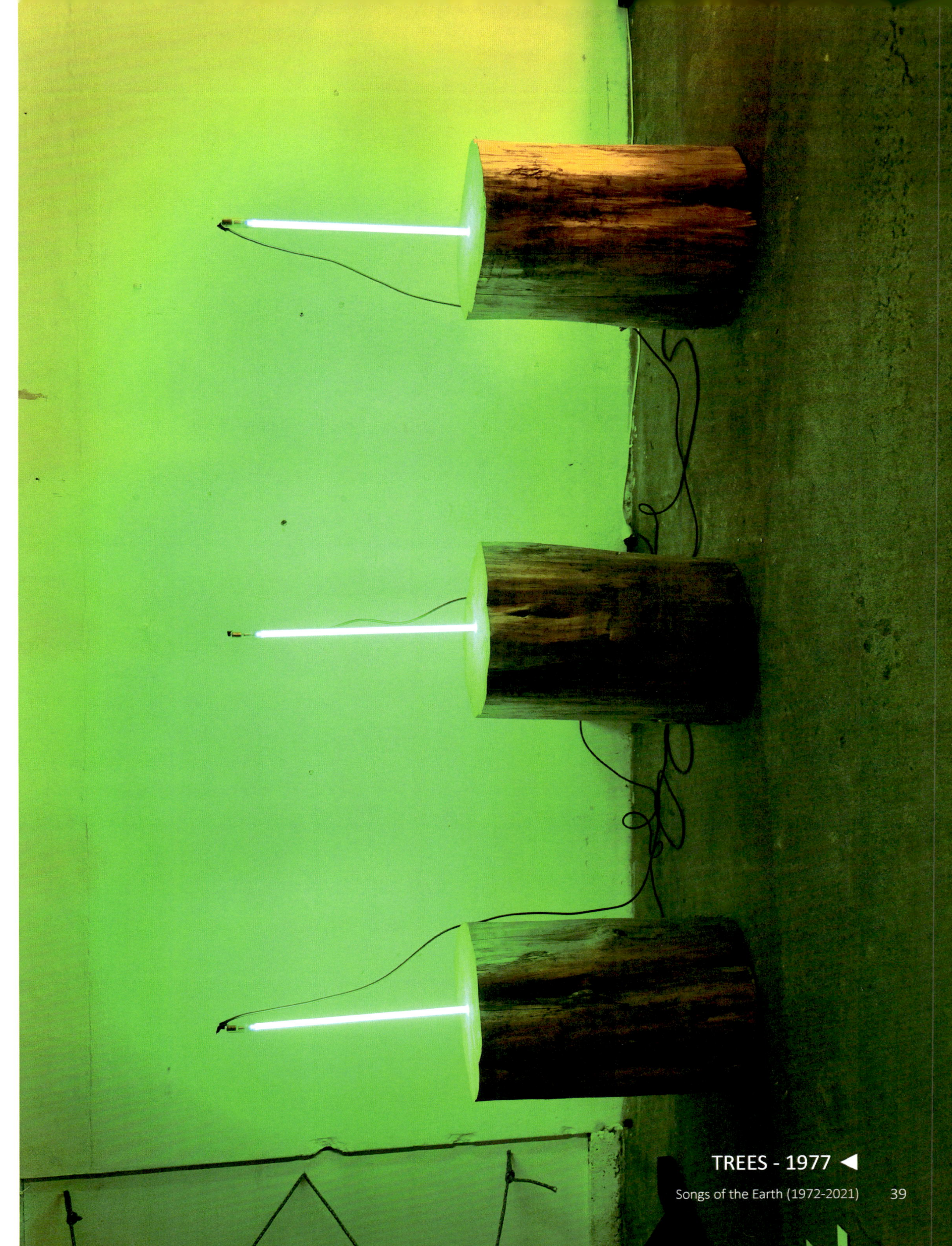



Songs of the Earth (1972-2021)    39

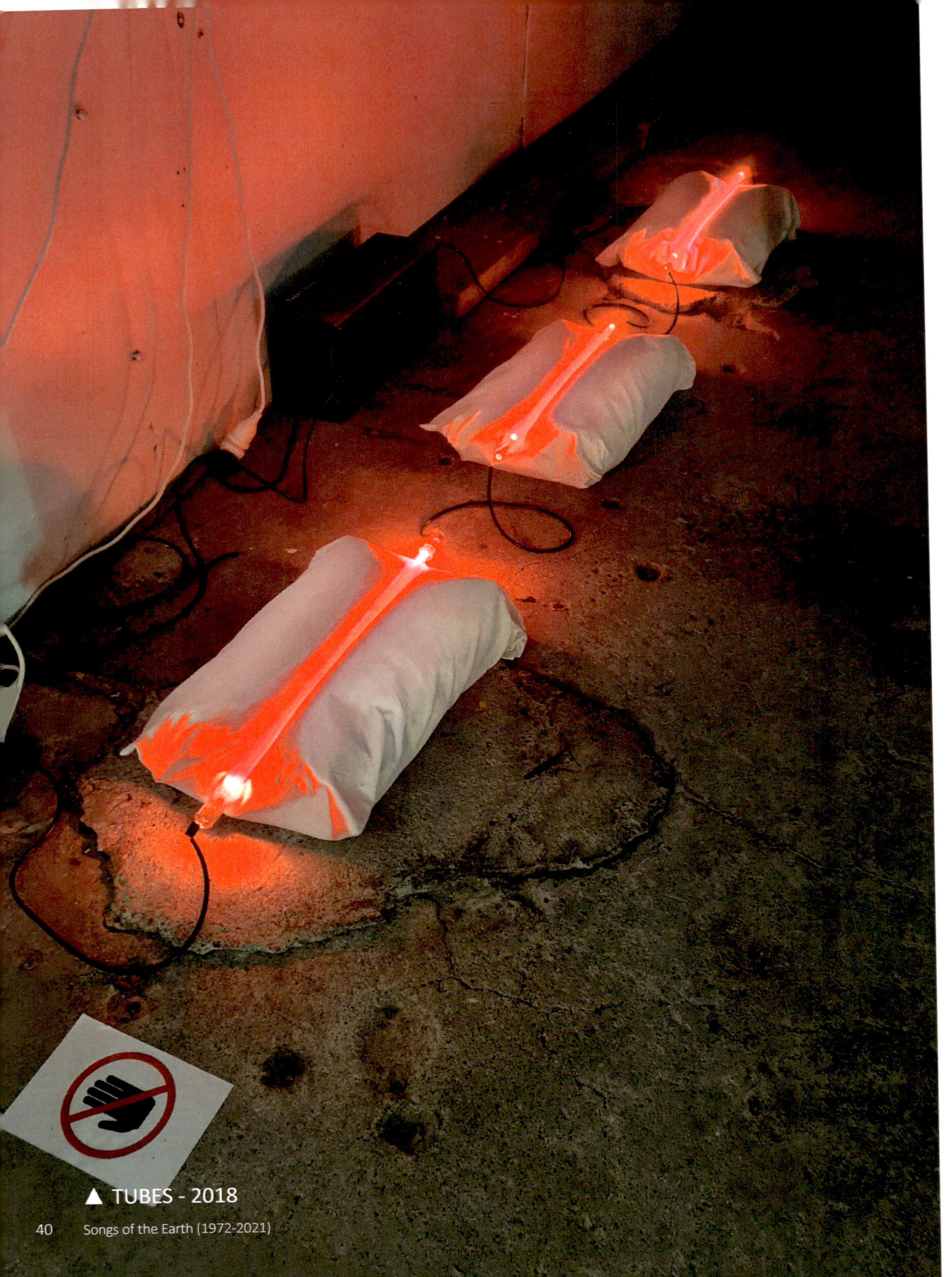


TUBES - 2018

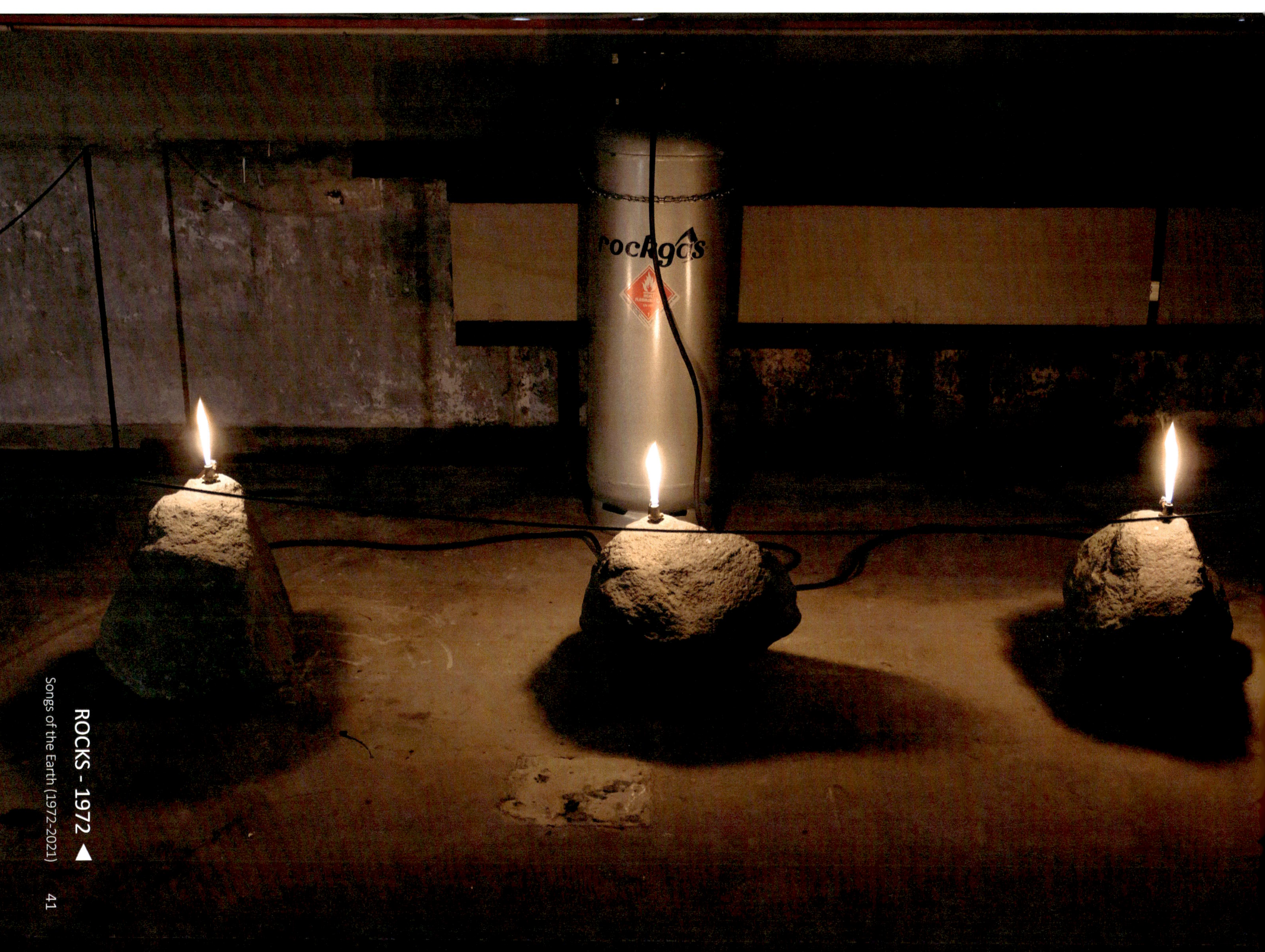


ROCKS - 1972 ▲

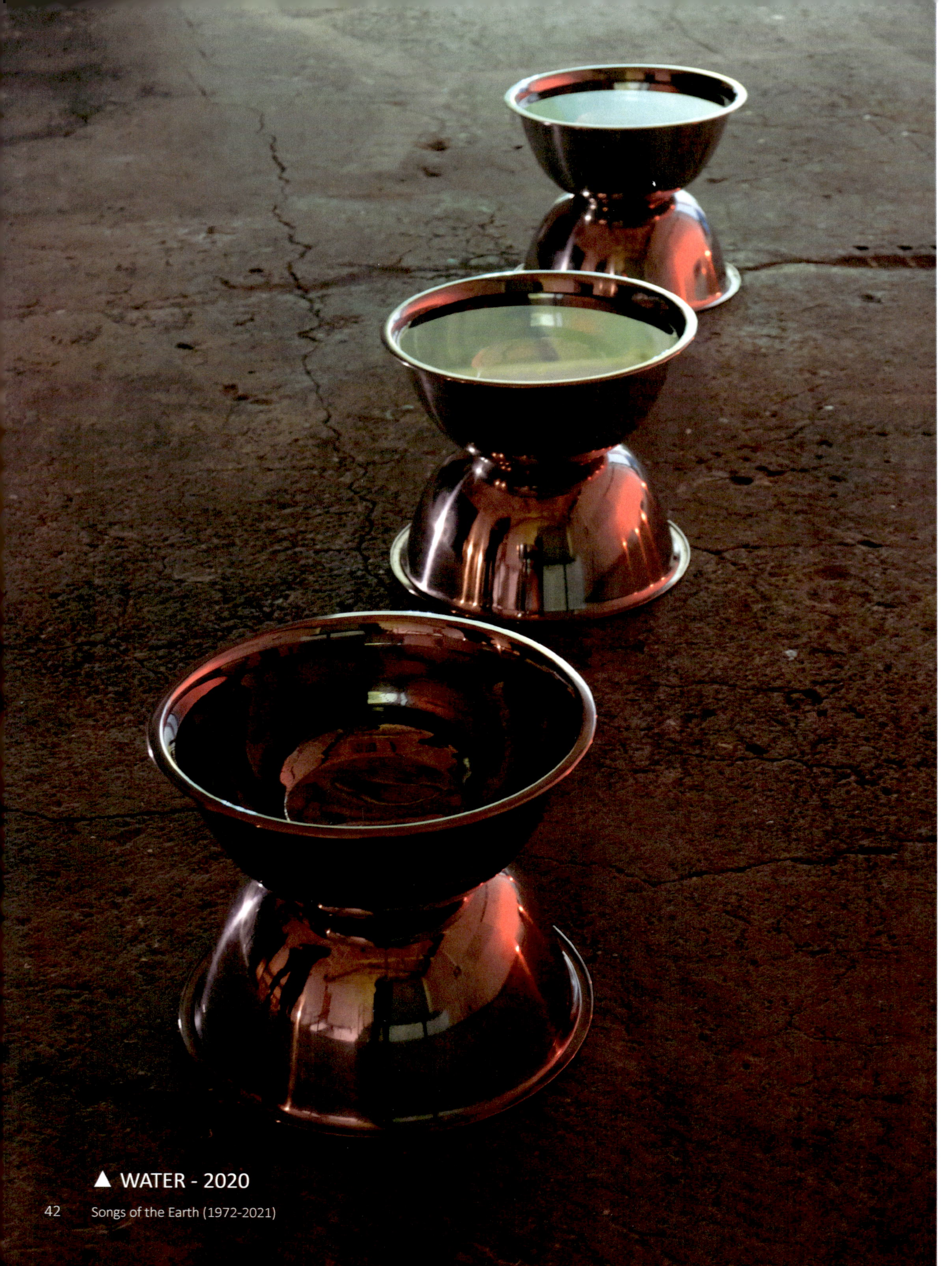

▲ WATER - 2020

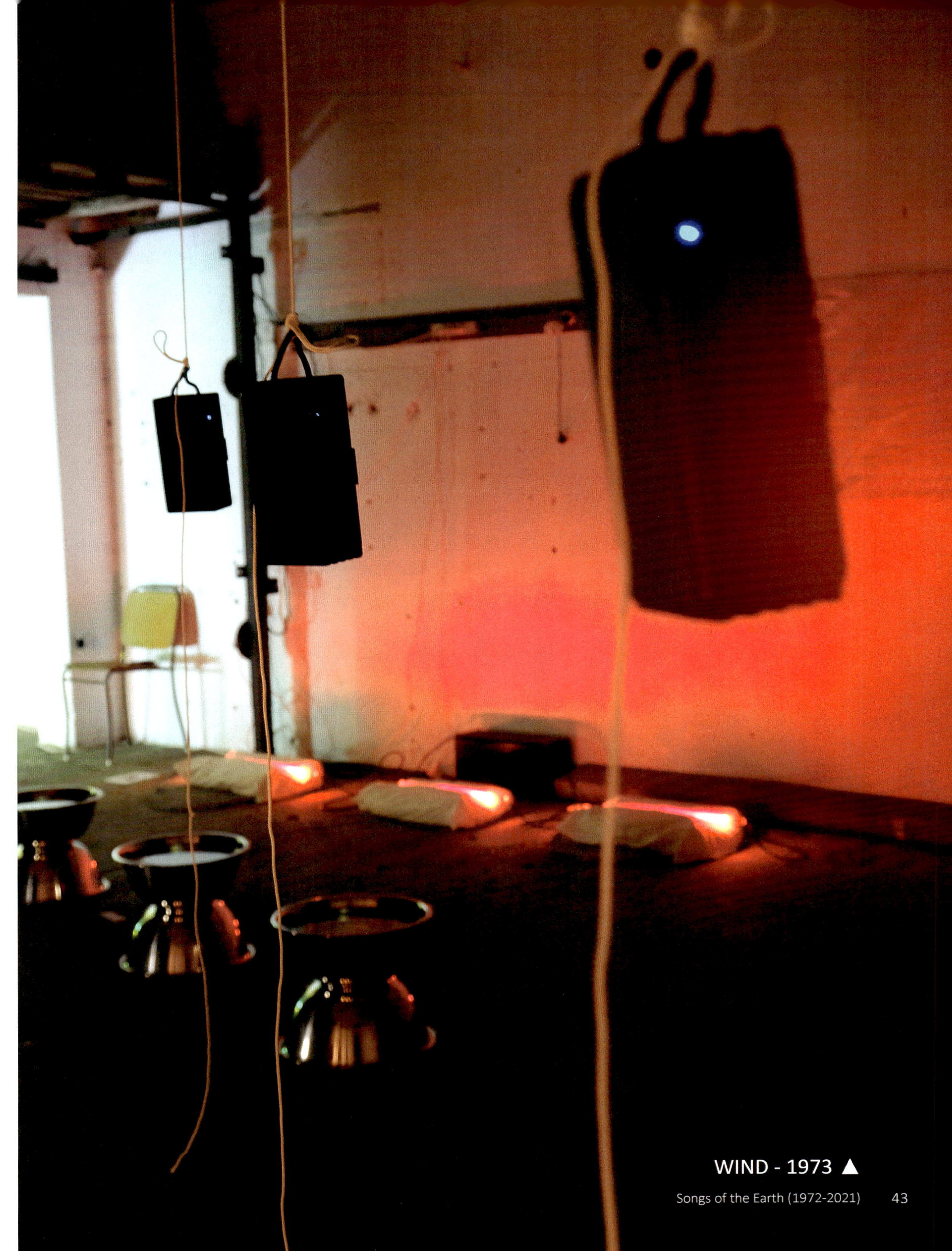

WIND - 1973 ▲

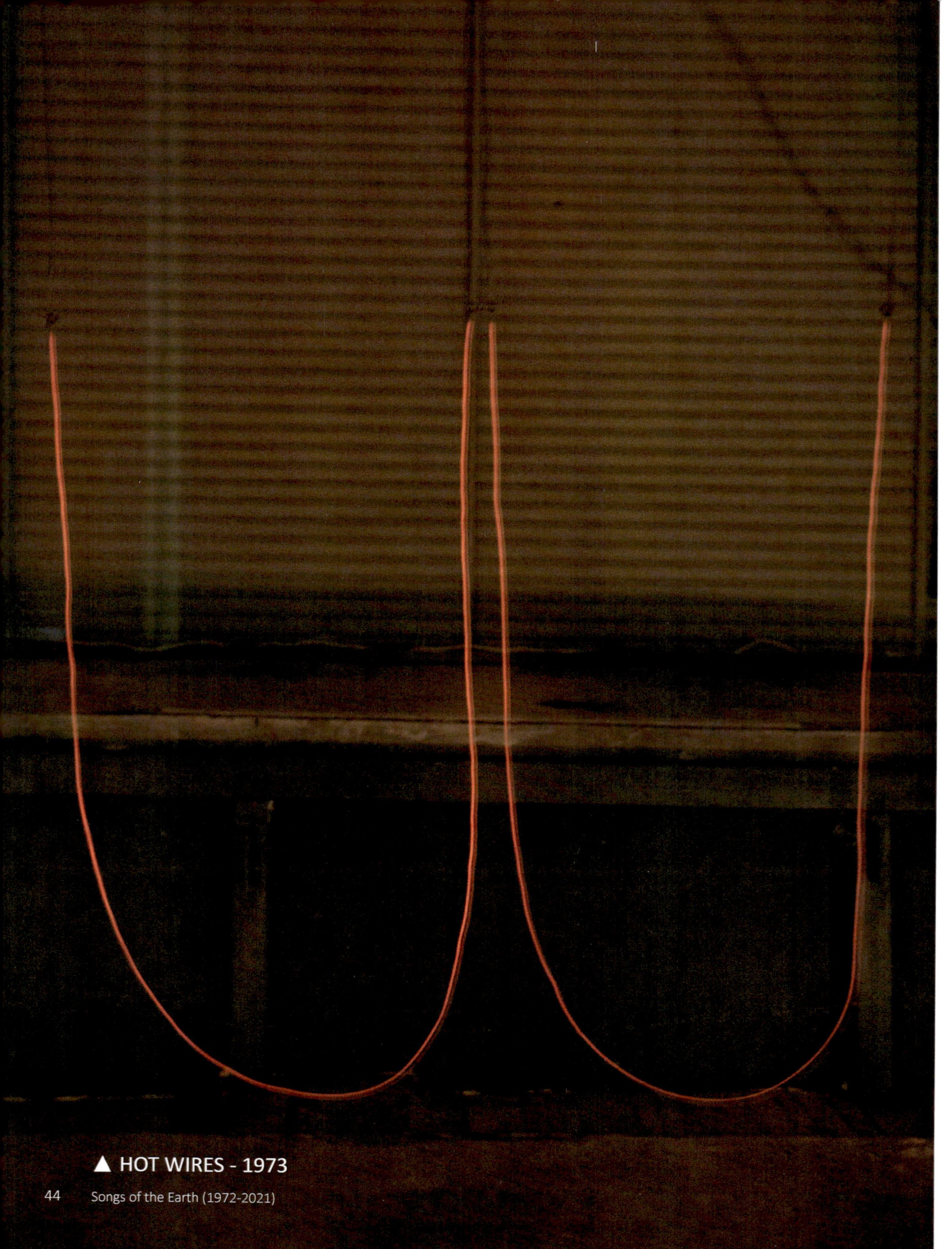

▲ HOT WIRES - 1973

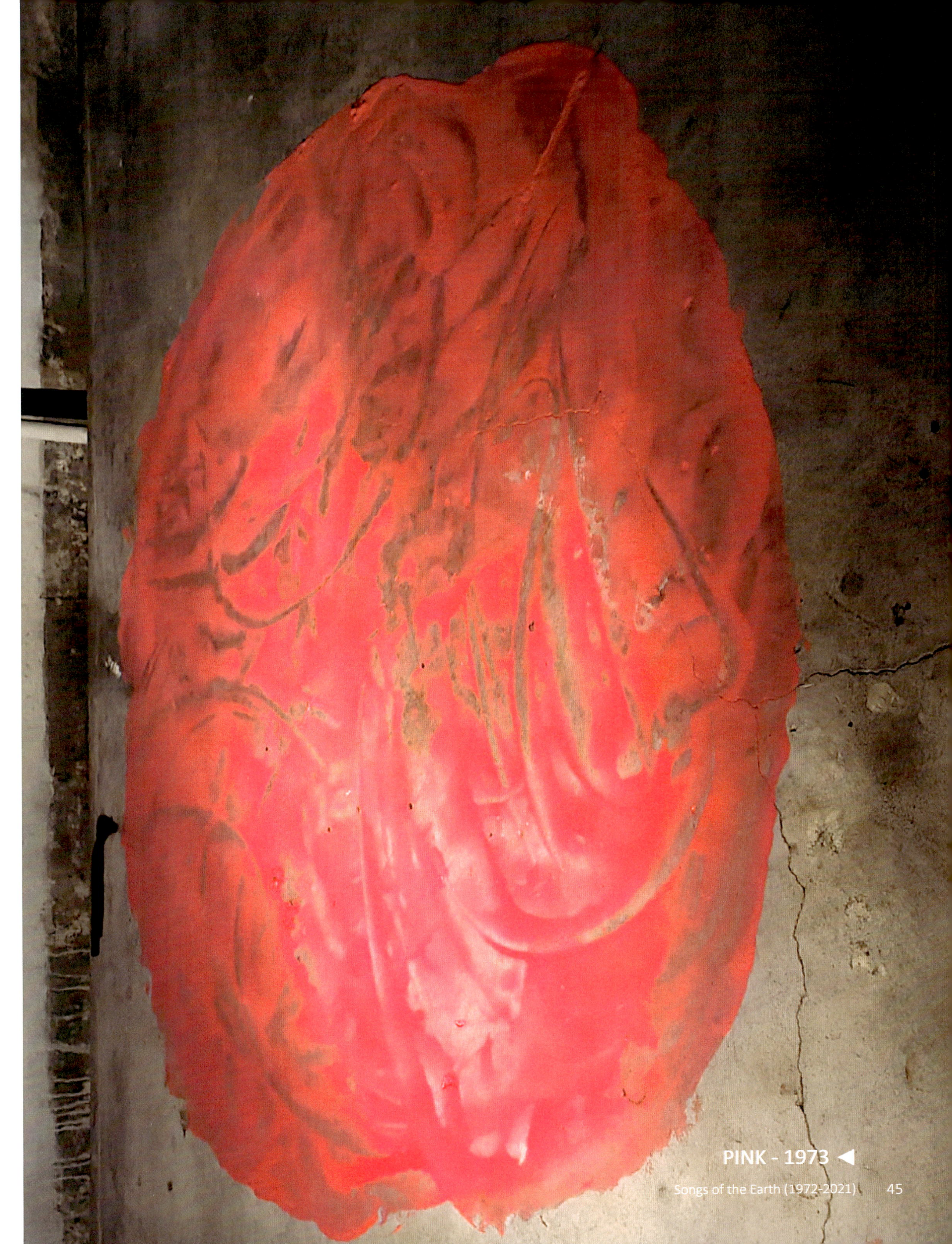

PINK - 1973 ◄

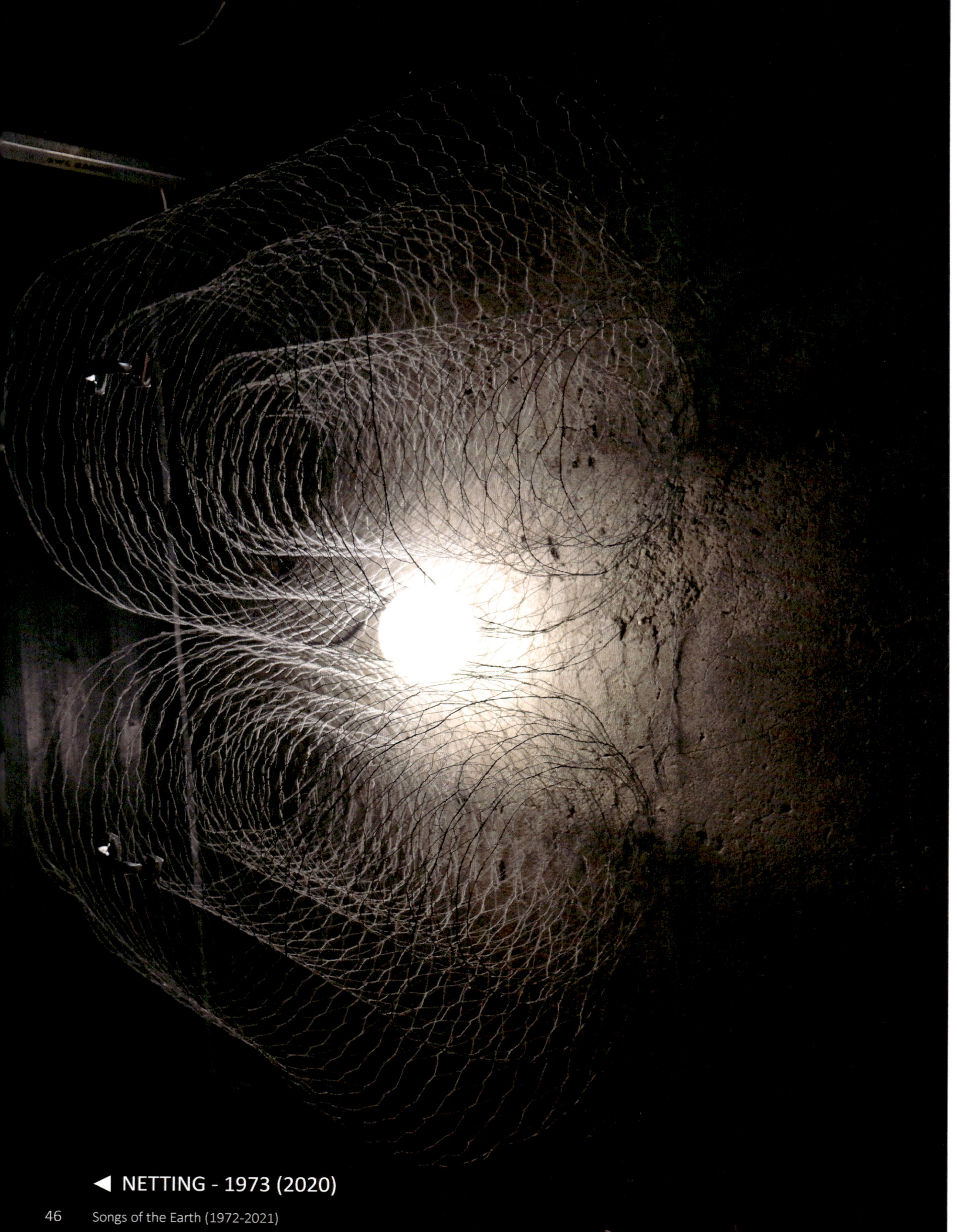

◀ NETTING - 1973 (2020)

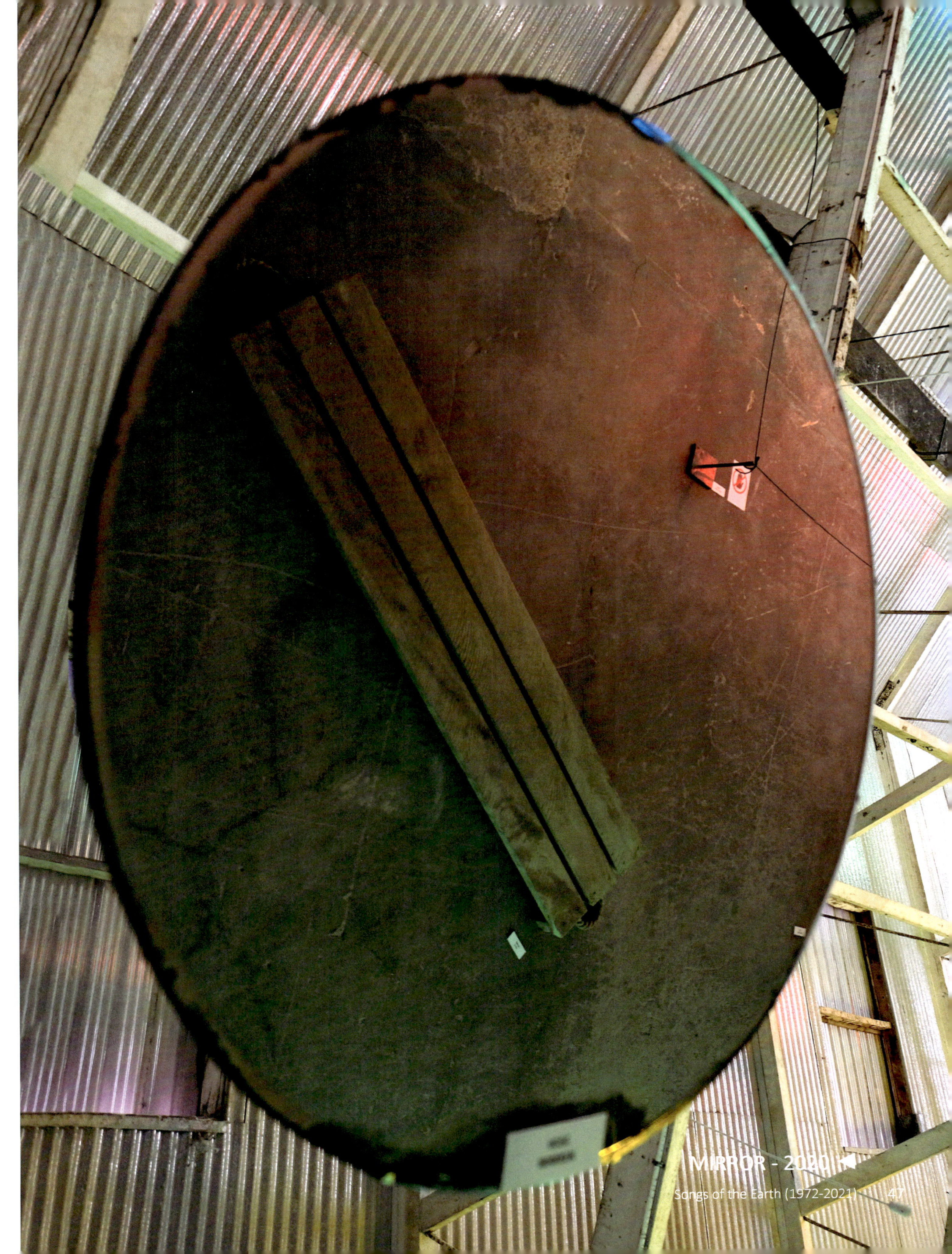
MIRROR - 2020
Songs of the Earth (1972-2021)     47

9 780473 602611